BAKERS' D

This book will give you a glimpse into the faith, due diligence, devotion and strength it takes to be called into the missionary field. I'm sure in writing this book there were many moments where my parents wish they could go back in time and handle situations differently, or make a different decision, but that is not what was asked of them. What was asked is that they handle each day with the love and wisdom that God had equipped them with in that moment, and that I believe they did every day. My life has been so richly blessed by the perseverance to remain consistent in God's will for their lives above all personal desires; what a gift to give a child. This is a book of sacrifice and blessings, joy and pain and no doubt a few "bad Jim Baker jokes." It may be missing a few stories of true patience with relation to their teenage daughter, but that is just another example of their incredible grace.

Lisa Chavez,
Their Proud Daughter

In 1975 Jim and Kay Baker decided they needed me in their lives. And 9 months later I was born on May 4 1976, two days before my mother's birthday. I was born into a family much bigger than expected and saw many faces as I grew up. We took several adventures with my parents as we saw the country on long family trips! I think of the movie "Vacation," but add 10 more kids and a van! Now as a father myself, I have no idea how they pulled that off without throwing us out of that van! Most of all I learned compassion and remember growing up watching intoxicated people come to our door. We were so scared of them but my parents would feed them, but I always kept an eye on my dad and he would pray with them! I'm blessed to have the greatest parents in my life with hearts for God.

David Baker,
Their Grateful Son

Jim and Kay Baker's book is not just many stories of "Navajoland." It is a strong story of faith and endurance through trials and situations. I count it an extreme honor to know this dedicated couple for almost four decades. As the former Editor of <u>Navajo Trails</u> and <u>Navajo Neighbors</u>, the ministry that Jim and Kay have led is not just another ministry. Their faith ... their perseverance ... their dedication to those less fortunate in the Four Corners area is unprecedented. I pray that this factual book inspires many more to be involved in assisting these "First Americans." Thank you, Jim and Kay Baker, for being on the very frontlines of ministry for four decades.

Rev. Bob Armstrong,
President of Love-Link Ministries

It truly has been a blessing to have worked and traveled with Jim and Kay Baker for over 20 years. We have learned so much from them as we observed their Christ-like lives. They have mentored us and if it wasn't for them we would not be where we are in our spiritual journey.

Joe and Gerri Begay, Pastors and Missionaries
Grace Fellowship Church, Chinle, Arizona

Although we hail from the same part of the country, Lancaster County, Pennsylvania, the Bakers and the Bombergers never crossed paths until God called each of us to Navajoland, where our love and ministries have brought us together and our friendship has grown. Jim and Kay Baker's life journey certainly is Proverbs 3:5 & 6, put into action. Fully "trusting in the LORD with all of their heart; not leaning on their own understanding, and in all of their ways acknowledging Him, for God has been faithful to direct their footsteps."

Larry Bomberger,
Chairman, Navajo Ministries Board
Director of Farmington Senior Center, 1988-2014

Krickitt and I are honored to be a part of this book and to have such a wonderful relationship with our friends Jim and Kay Baker. It is a true blessing to see the passion and inspiration of Jim and Kay. The results of their work that they have put forward in their quest blessed by God has enabled them to change the lives of many. Our community, this state and even our world is a better place because of people like Jim and Kay, who have dedicated their lives to making a difference in the lives of others.

**Kim and Krickitt Carpenter,
Co-Authors of "The Vow,"
Inspiration for the major motion picture.
Kim is also C.E.O. of San Juan County, New Mexico**

A Divine appointment ... that would describe the day Kay Baker arrived at my front door, just to talk. It's been nearly 35 years ago now, so the details are fuzzy. What I do remember is an instant recognition that God would use her, her family and Navajo Ministries to touch our lives in an extraordinary way! As author Debbie McComber would say, "God's fingerprints were all over that intersection of time and eternity." In nearly 35 years, our families have been interconnected ... in good times and hard times, making wonderful memories. We Fitzs are eternally grateful for the fellowship and friendship we share with Bakers.

**Bob and Leslie Fitz,
Former houseparents and long-time friends**

It has been my wonderful privilege to have known Jim and Kay Baker since they came to Farmington. It has always impressed me that they left a comfortable life and living to come to Northern New Mexico to work with children and families in such great need. They have given their lives to serve others and have worked tirelessly to help grow Navajo Ministries into one of the most well-respected organizations in the country. They are hardworking, conscientious, professionals and "heroes of the faith." We praise God for their compassion and are deeply grateful for their sacrifices and commitment to so many people.

Ronna Jordan,
Founder and President of Houses with Hope

Jim and Kay Baker have an amazing love for children. We had the opportunity to witness their love for children first-hand while we served on their staff as houseparents. They have wonderful stories to tell of their many years of experience both as houseparents and as leaders at Navajo Ministries. We now have the awesome privilege of being their pastors. Their commitment to ministry to the children of Navajo Ministries and their leadership is outstanding. We are also glad to know them as our friends.

Randy Joslin, Lead Pastor of Oasis Ministries,
Farmington, New Mexico
Debbie Joslin, Executive Director,
Grace Place Pregnancy and Health Center

Jim Baker and his wife Kay were called by God to be servants to the Navajo Nation. With God's directive, they have given a meaningful purpose to impact many lives for the kingdom of God. One afternoon as I was driving home in the early eighties, Jim was sharing the word of salvation during his "Going Home" radio show. I had heard of Jesus before, and sometimes attended church, but the Holy Spirit touched my heart in a very strong way there in my vehicle and I gave my life to Jesus to be my Savior and Lord.

Since then, I got married, and my beautiful wife, Barbara, and I have spent 33 years working side by side and raising three children, Myles, Melissa and Mark, with the knowledge of Jesus Christ. God has blessed me with an art talent and my wife Barbara and I have opened a few art galleries in the Four

Corners area. I also served three terms on the board. We give God all the glory for placing people, like Jim and Kay Baker, in our path to help us grow in our walk with God and fulfill our destiny in Him.

Mark Silversmith,
Navajo Artist

After serving 12 years as Mayor of Farmington, I'm blessed with memories and lifelong friendships from those years in office, many who stand out for their contributions to the community financially, or through years of volunteerism and sometimes both. Jim and Kay Baker fall into a category all their own, they have given their "Hearts and Souls" to helping children receive a good start in life, and they reach far into the community providing prayer and assistance to others. How does a community recognize individuals who give like that?

The Chamber of Commerce, at their annual banquet recognizes individuals for their outstanding achievements and dedication to the community. In 2001 the Bakers were selected to receive the Chamber's prized award as "Humanitarians of the Year." It is a very competitive field to have been selected for this honor but Jim and Kay were unanimously selected for a lot of reasons. Finally; a way to say, "Thank you."

Giving heart and soul doesn't stop there. Jim is also with his community out front on the National Day of Prayer, Day of Remembrance and Memorial Day and on other memorable days. Jim joined a group of citizens in front of City Hall at the flag pole just days after 9-11, leading us in prayer for those who lost their lives in the Twin Towers. It's not hard to remember the good things the Bakers do. "That's just what they do," all the time.

Bill Standley,
City of Farmington Mayor, 1998 to 2010

Upon arriving to the Four Corners area in April 1996, my wife Rose and I met Jim Baker and his wife Kay at Navajo Ministries in Farmington, New Mexico. We were just starting the Victory Life Church and rehab home in Shiprock, New Mexico. We let Jim know about us and he gladly offered that Navajo Ministries would provide us with financial support on a monthly basis. Throughout the years they helped us by donating a van and mobile home, too. Jim has helped us network and connect us with ministries and churches in the area as we've done Vacation Bible Schools and other activities. He is truly a servant of the Lord Jesus. We are thankful for Navajo Ministries' support, prayers and help in providing service to the Navajo people.

**Pastor Robert Tso,
Victory Life Church, Shiprock, New Mexico**

When I was Chairman of the Board for several years, founder Jack Drake and I would meet Saturday mornings to pray for the Ministry. Jack prayed repeatedly that the Lord would send someone to be a dedicated worker with a vision for the future and eventually become President and accomplish more than he had. That prayer was answered in 1975 when He sent Jim and Kay Baker as houseparents. When Jack retired in 1987, Jim was elected President and expanded the vision greater than we ever expected. I no longer live in Farmington but I am still an enthusiastic supporter of Navajo Ministries.

**Dick Ullrich,
Retired, living in Indiana**

THE BAKERS' DOZEN
—AND THEN SOME—

FOUR DECADES OF ADVENTURES IN NAVAJOLAND

JIM AND KAY BAKER

XULON PRESS

ACKNOWLEDGMENTS

"Thank you" are such simple words to be used when expressing appreciation to those who have provided assistance, encouragement, wisdom and honest opinions as we have taken on this major task of highlighting our 40 years of ministry at Navajo Ministries. We are so grateful to the following people who have helped bring this story to the printed pages of this book:

Our natural children, Lisa and David, you shared our successes and failures, and still love us. The dozens of Navajo children who came into our home, you provided us with adventures and wonderful memories, some of which have made it to the pages of this book.

Special houseparents and other staff members who continue to be treasured friends, you know who you are. It has been our privilege to grieve with your sorrows and celebrate in your joys over the years.

Bob Armstrong, former editor of Navajo Trails and Navajo Neighbors publications. Your writings over the years provided us with some of the details that we needed when our memories failed. You prodded us to write our story. Here it is!

Leslie Fitz, friend and special sister in the Lord, you encouraged us to squeeze our feelings and descriptions out of our experiences and onto the printed pages that follow.

Eric Fisher, former newspaper journalist and incoming President of Navajo Ministries. Your writing and editing skills have been so helpful with our written presentations over the years. And, that includes your editing of this book.

Kelly Karlin, Director of Administration at Navajo Ministries, who has a keen eye for details, you have carefully made sure we got every jot and tittle correct.

Hannah Rodden, Graphic Designer at Navajo Ministries, you took our Bakers' Dozen theme and transformed it into a fantastic facsimile of our family in our early years, producing an attractive book cover.

Xulon Press, thank you for making our story a printed reality.

TABLE OF CONTENTS

DEDICATION

This book is dedicated, first of all, to our Lord Jesus Christ, who gave us a story ... His story of redemption, life and purpose that we were able to live out among our many friends in Navajoland. Without His calling in our lives, we would have missed out on so many blessings.

We are so thankful for our parents who introduced us to our Savior. Our siblings were also an important part of our growth and development as we learned to share our toys, bedrooms, and abundant life experiences. Bob, Mary Elizabeth, Gene, Dan, Judy, Donna and Parke: many thanks for the wonderful, loving interaction as siblings. Those childhood experiences played an important part in our desire to provide a fun-loving atmosphere for other children who were not as fortunate as we were growing up.

There's no way we could write a book about our years at Navajo Ministries without sharing the impact that Jack Drake, the founder, had in our lives. From the moment Rev. James Snare shared Navajo Missions with us, we wanted to meet this man of faith that began a home for children in a borrowed tent. As we joined with Jack in ministry, he became our mentor and "mission-field dad." What a privilege it has been to follow in his footsteps and carry on his vision into the 21st century.

Our home church, First Church of God, in Lancaster, Pennsylvania, provided us with vital spiritual growth and development. So many of your faces come to our minds when we think about our Sunday School classes, Junior Church services, Christian Endeavor gatherings, Vacation Bible Schools and Youth groups. When we shared our calling to Navajo Missions with you in 1975, you whole-heartily committed monthly missionary support for us that has continued through four decades!

While we dedicated our natural children, Lisa and David, to the Lord when they were small, it is our privilege to dedicate this book to them now. Lisa and David, you were "missionaries without a choice" as we fulfilled God's call in our lives. You were forced to share mom and dad with 33 other children who came to live in our home. While we had our rough times, we have had far more enjoyable times. We managed to hold fast to one another and see God meet our every need. We are proud to be your parents.

Grandchildren ... what a gift they are to grandparents! We get to love them and then send them back to their parents. Jami and Lisa, it was such a privilege it was to have Breann in our lives for three years. She remains forever in our hearts and we look forward to being with her in Heaven. Dave and Heather, you have given us two beautiful granddaughters, Seattle and Samantha. They continue to be the joy of our lives as we watch them grow and develop. Thank you for sharing them with us.

We also recognize the many Navajo boys and girls who lived with us during our years of houseparenting.

Without them, we would not have put this book together and called it "The Bakers' Dozen." To each of you, we say "thank you" for being a special part of our lives. We learned so much from all of you and hope you have many happy memories to reflect upon. Now, in our later years, it is always our joy to see you come for visits and introduce us to your children. They, too, hold a special place in our hearts.

And, this is a great place to express our thanks and appreciation to our wonderful staff who, over the years, assisted us in providing hope and restoration to our Navajo neighbors. It takes many hearts and hands to provide services to those who come in our doors, or turn on the radio, looking for love and acceptance. Whether you served for a few months, or several decades, you have touched the lives of so many people. Thank you for your faithfulness, tenacity, and dedication to the Lord. Together, we have seen lives changed for eternity.

Finally, this book is dedicated to our countless friends who have prayed for and provided donations to this ministry over the past four decades while we have served here. None of what you read on these pages would be possible without your faithfulness and sacrifice. Thank you for joining with us in reaching our Navajo neighbors with the love of Christ. To God be the glory!

INTRODUCTION

Whe God came knocking on our hearts' doors in 1974, we were content being near our families and friends. Lancaster County was our home. I loved my job working as a door-to-door salesman with the Fuller Brush Company. Our church was a focal point of our spiritual growth and development. We lived in a new home that was completed just after our marriage in 1969. Kay and I were so happy with our new life together being parents to a little girl named Lisa.

But, then God started "messing with us." Who would have thought that attending a Sunday night missions program at church would disrupt our comfortable life in Pennsylvania Dutch country? But that was the beginning of an adventure that would take us 2,000 miles across the country to Navajoland. Only God could bring that kind of change into our lives. Only God would be able to jolt us out of our comfort zone. And, only God would choose someone like me to uproot our family and move into the unknown.

This story is really not "our story." It's His story lived out in our lives. In reality it's also a "His-tory" of the past four decades of our lives. I invite you to come along for the adventure. I think we have a little bit of everything tucked away within these chapters. If you ever thought about taking a missions trip or becoming a missionary, look out! This could be the door that will open for you to begin praying about that possibility. If you think that God could never use you because of lack of experience, Bible knowledge, your age or whatever else you come up with, I invite you to begin reading this story. He has a place picked out for all kinds of people. You just need to walk through that door.

Perhaps you picked up this book because you thought the picture on the cover was cute. Maybe you were drawn to the Native American look of the drawing. Maybe you have a love for children and a desire to help those who are disadvantaged. These are some more good reasons to get into this book. You will learn much about the Navajo, the largest Nation of American Indians in our country. You will also discover how Navajo Ministries has been a part of restoring hope and restoration to families since 1953.

I encourage you to slip into our journey and walk along with us as we take you through the valleys and mountain tops of life on the mission field. You will find that we have had our share of disappointments and challenges. That happens whether you're a missionary or not. We have also seen tremendous victories during these past 40 years. It is our desire that you will exit this story and realize that God is good all the time, and all the time – God is good!

Jim Baker

When we were living in Pennsylvania and seeking God's will for our lives, I knew God was calling me to work with children. One night I talked with Jim about

xx

doing foster care in our home. We had the extra room and there certainly was a need in our area. Jim's response was, "No, we can't do that. You'll have kids coming for a short time and then leaving us, and you'll be crying all the time." So, what do we do? We move 2,000 miles away and have foster children come in and out of our home for 15 years! He was right ... I had my share of tears when children left our home.

The words you read in italics in this book are my words, reflecting upon the many rewarding and challenging experiences we had in those years of raising children, and the years that followed. *We continue to be blessed by the friendships of our natural children, Lisa and David, as well as many of our foster children who are now adults. The camaraderie of our Navajo Ministries team, whether former staff or present, continues to be a gift in our lives every day.*

We are living proof that God can use <u>anyone</u>. And when He calls, He equips us. "Now may the God of peace, who brought up from the dead our Lord Jesus, the great Shepherd of the sheep, and ratified an eternal covenant with His blood, may He equip you with all you need for doing His will. May He produce in you, through the power of Jesus Christ, every good thing that is pleasing to Him. All glory to him forever and ever! Amen." (Hebrews 13: 20, 21 NLT)

Kay Baker

Chapter One

GO WEST YOUNG FAMILY

It was April Fool's Day in 1975. This day is known for silly pranks and less than truthful statements to our friends and families. On this particular April 1st, there were some who were convinced that *we* were fools as we packed our lives and our possessions into a used Ford van and U-Haul trailer and headed west.

God's call in our lives was clear. Had we not responded to Him in a positive way, *we would have been* the fools. And He would have called someone else to serve Him in Navajoland. How thankful I am, four decades later, that we obeyed His call.

It was the day after Easter. Kay and I and our 3-year-old daughter, Lisa, along with our long-haired dachshund, Gretel, gathered at the front of my parents' home on Rohrerstown Road in Lancaster, Pennsylvania. Family members provided final hugs and best wishes. Prayers were offered by our pastor. And then we climbed into our van and carefully pulled out of the driveway.

Tears streamed down the cheeks of many. Lisa asked Kay why she was crying. "We will miss our family," Kay said, tearfully. Lisa quickly responded, "Don't cry mommy, we'll come back to visit." As I glanced in the rearview mirror at the waving hands of our family, a lump took up residence in my throat, realizing we were headed out on a life-changing adventure–one that would be quite different from what we experienced so far in Lancaster County.

As we began our travels, we shared highlights of our trip on a cassette recorder, to later share with our family. We called our adventure, "Voyage of the Victory Van." Our friends and family made sure Lisa would have something to look forward to each day as we headed across the country. A box full of individually wrapped gifts included snacks, games, handmade cards and coloring books.

At one point Lisa asked, "Dad, do you know there is a red truck following us?" As I looked in the rearview mirror, I smiled, realizing it was the U-Haul trailer attached to the back of our van. On the second night of staying at a motel, I managed to get the van and trailer rig trapped in the rear parking area. The more I tried to back that trailer out of captivity, the more ensnared I became. Fortunately, a truck driver saw my plight, took over the wheel and quickly had me headed in the right direction.

I felt like a mini truck driver myself as I maneuvered our eight-passenger van and dual-axel U-Haul trailer across the country. Having never pulled a trailer before, I found the crowded rush hour streets and highways to be quite challenging. I was even pulled over by the police in St. Louis, the Gateway to the West, for going too slow during their rush hour. But, we had precious cargo that needed to reach our destination in New Mexico.

The green hills and valleys leveled off to the flat-lands of Kansas. Huge tractors were crawling over the land, tilling and planting the crops for another season. Farmhouses and barns sporadically appeared in the midst of the fields, providing homesteads for these hardworking families. It was in one of those homes where we would spend the night.

The Clayton Peck family lived in the area called Yates Center. They were dirt farmers who invited us to spend the night as we made our way west. Clayton was on the National Missions committee for the Churches of God in North America. I'll share more about our connection with the Pecks later. Lisa enjoyed stretching her legs while chasing a calf around their yard. Clayton found out that Kay was directionally challenged when he told her to sit at the north end of the table for a scrumptious meat and potatoes meal.

As we made our way to bed that Saturday night, it was a bit crowded with all three of us and Gretel sharing the same double bed. We were tired after a long day. Even the howling coyotes didn't keep us awake. The next morning we had the opportunity to share in their church service. The church was small. There was a total of 22 of us there. They had an adult and children's Sunday School class. Lisa was joined by two other kids in the children's class. She held her nose through most of the service. The scent of the cattle farmers was something new to her.

The next morning we headed down the long farm lane and made our way to Interstate 70. We soon realized that Kansas is a long, flat state. You can drive all day and still be in Kansas. There was one place in the state we needed to visit. Great Bend is just 75 miles from the center of America. But, that's not why we headed there.

It was the home base of the Fuller Brush Company factory. After spending 10 years as one of their leading salesmen in Pennsylvania, I just had to see where all those mops, brooms and brushes I sold were made. It was the final chapter in our life as we once knew it. The time had come to stop knocking on wooden doors and trust God to open new doors of opportunity that would lead us to ministry with the Navajo.

As we aimed our van and trailer into a stiff headwind, the clouds darkened. Huge rolling tumble weeds scurried across the highway like giant hedgehogs sliding across a slippery floor. Large rain drops turned into a downpour, which soon became a pelting hail storm. And then, in the middle of the afternoon, fog rolled across the plains, obstructing our view. We definitely weren't in Pennsylvania anymore … this was Kansas!

The clouds began to clear as we neared the Colorado border. For nearly a hundred miles we were reminded on huge billboards that Prairie Dog Town and Rattlesnake Pit were just ahead. It was something that any new traveler to the west would want to see–at least I did. After seeing how much they wanted to charge us for a peek at a sleeping snake and a miniature groundhog, we decided to just get gas and be on our way to Colorado.

While the landscape of eastern Colorado looked a lot like the rest of Kansas, we could begin to see the purple hue of the Rockies in the distance. Our gaze was interrupted, however, when the sliding passenger door of our van blew open at 55 mph! Lisa was strapped in securely, so all was well, although one of our potted plants nearly tumbled to the road.

"Welcome to colorful Colorado" read the sign as we cruised along through the eastern plains. At this point it

wasn't that colorful. The van began to groan a bit as we climbed in elevation. Our first dust storm blew across the highway, causing what looked like a brown fog to slow the traffic. Little did we know then that we would see many more dust storms roll through our lives in New Mexico.

The headwind, combined with the increasing elevation, sucked a lot more gas out of our van than expected. And we were learning in the west there aren't gas stations every 10 miles or so. We were running on fumes when we rolled into the little gas station just off the Interstate. From now on we would fill up the tank when the gauge got to the half-way mark.

As we headed to Colorado Springs, a light snow shower blurred our view of Pikes Peak. It was the tallest mountain we had ever seen at more than 14,000 feet above sea level. This unsettled weather caused us to have second thoughts about heading through the mountains of Southwestern Colorado to our final destination in Farmington, New Mexico. So, we decided to play it safe and head south to Albuquerque, even though it added over 200 miles to our trip.

"Welcome to New Mexico, Land of Enchantment" was the official greeting on the large yellow sign as we headed south. We were now in our tenth state on our "Voyage of the Victory Van." The ribbon of highway took us through breath-taking scenery, which included herds of antelope and mule deer grazing near the flowing streams and rivers. Our final night of the trip had us sleeping in what many believe is the oldest town in America, Santa Fe, New Mexico.

As we awoke to a covering of snow on the adobe buildings, pine trees and yucca plants, it was like God had given us a fresh new view of our calling to the Navajo.

The swirling winds, dust, rain and hail had gone away. It was a new day in New Mexico. It was also the first day of the rest of our lives.

We headed to Albuquerque and then west on Interstate 40 to Gallup. It was there we called Jack Drake, the founder and President of the mission, to give him an update on our travels. His deep voice brought comfort to me when he expressed his joy that we were nearing our new "home."

We were now just 125 miles from Farmington. The stark desert land scattered with occasional octagon shaped log dwellings with dirt floors, called hogans, were home to many Navajo families in the 1970s. Lone sheep herders, accompanied by a couple of dogs, were seen at times, too, as we made our way past the Shiprock pinnacle rising 1,700 feet off the desert floor. This land was home to the largest tribe of Native Americans in our country. Before long, we would make this area our home, too.

At the top of the long hill that drops down into the city of Farmington, we noticed the sign that says, "Welcome to Farmington." For a moment, Kay and I looked at each other and together wondered, "What are we doing here?" Did we really hear God call us to this desolate, high-desert land 2,000 miles away from our family and friends in the green rolling hills of Pennsylvania?

We forced the dark clouds of doubt out of our minds and headed on remembering one of the verses we memorized as children. "Now faith is the substance of things hoped for, the evidence of things not seen." (Hebrews 11:1) We didn't know what the future held, but we knew *who* held our future. We knew there would be new friends, new housing, new experiences and new challenges as we continued to serve our faithful friend, Jesus, who is the same yesterday, today and forever. What about those "yesterdays" in our lives? What were our childhoods like? Who impacted us to one day step out in faith and invest our hopes and dreams into the lives of those we know today as our Navajo neighbors? Our story is *His* story. We invite you to come along with us as we reflect on the ups and downs and twists and turns of life that we have experienced during these past four decades at Navajo Ministries.

Chapter Two

THE BABY OF THE FAMILY

I was the last child of six born to Roy and Esther Baker. However, I was the first of their children born in a hospital. Well, just barely. I remember mom relating the story that she didn't quite make it into the delivery room. While on a gurney in the hallway of Lancaster General Hospital, with a janitor standing by with a mop, she gave birth to me, James David Baker.

On March 1, 1947 I made my entrance into this world. It was certainly a different world from what we are accustomed to today. You could buy a new car for $1,300 and a new house for $6,600. A gallon of gas was just 15 cents and a postage stamp was 3 cents. It was the year that the sound barrier was first broken and way out in Roswell, New Mexico there was a UFO incident that created a great deal of interest. Even today, this town draws many tourists to check it out.

My siblings included Bob, the first born, in 1933. A year later sister Mary came along, and then Gene in 1936. Three years later Dan joined the family and then another girl, Judy, was born in 1944. Finally, I became the "baby" of the family.

Our home was located on Rohrerstown Road, which was about three miles west of the city of Lancaster, Pennsylvania. Many tourists are familiar with our county since it is the home to Pennsylvania Dutch country, where more than 16,000 Amish call home. Most of the Amish lived on their farms on the rolling hills east of the city, so we didn't experience the hordes of visitors that poured into our area each year. We lived in a two-story brick home that my parents purchased for $5,000 in 1939. There were plenty of bedrooms and lots of grass for our big family to enjoy.

Judy was nearly 3 years old when I was born. It was that summer she became ill. At least it was then mom and dad first realized she had a large protrusion in her tummy. Tests soon provided the news that Judy had cancer. After several surgeries the cancer spread to her lungs and took her young life in October. I only remember seeing one picture of her holding me on a little wooden rocker. My sister, Mary, remembers Judy loving to sing "Jesus Loves Me" with great gusto. Mary said during Judy's hospitalization there was a quarantine due to scarlet fever, which meant no visitors. The nurses would hold Judy up to the window so we kids could wave to her.

Mary remembers that even with all the stress and anxiety of having a seriously ill child and caring for a new baby, mom and dad were strong and managed to keep the household going. She said, "Mom had an inner strength. Dad was a good supporter. They both put their trust in God. It was said over and over again, that although we had the pain of losing a dear daughter and sister, it was dispelled by the new life in Jimmy. It helped to chase the dark clouds away."

A few years before Judy was born, Great Aunt Emma, my dad's aunt, needed a place to live. She was only 50 years old and was considering living in a retirement home. Dad and mom would have nothing of that and invited her to live in our home. She provided the extra hands and feet to help our busy family. One of my earliest memories is of her pulling me in the little red wagon to the stream about a half mile down the road.

Aunt Emma, as we called her, was quite the chef when it came to making leftovers look like an entirely new meal. It's amazing how good Spam and potato cakes can taste when added to fresh vegetables. She added lots of happy moments to our home. I enjoyed making her laugh to the extent that, in her later years, she would sometimes laugh so hard, the "tears" would run down her leg!

Besides helping with our family, Aunt Emma made disposable cancer pads for hospitals and nursing homes. Aunt Emma was provided pads made from sheets of newspaper and covered with plastic. Her job was to hand stitch cotton fabric on top of the plastic, thereby making a disposable bed pad for patients. It's hard to know how many hundreds of these pads she made over the years. She also spent time embroidering pillow cases for family members and friends. Her embroidery work was amazing and we are glad to have one of her pieces hanging in our home today.

Aunt Emma was rarely sick and was still in our home when I graduated from high school. And, she was still there when I got married. My parents were beginning to think she would outlive them! Finally, at 99 years, after a faithful life of service, she went home to be with her

Father in heaven. She was just what my parents needed as they carried on the work of the farm while having this "Jimmy, come lately" in the family who needed care after school. In many ways Aunt Emma was like a second mom to me. Later on I would remember her role in my life as Kay and I became houseparents to children who would also need a second mom and dad.

My parents were always ready to welcome folks into their home. When I was a teen, David Heisey, my uncle's young son, needed a place to stay during the week. So, in a way, David became my younger brother for a while. Whenever there were evangelists or missionaries speaking at the church, our home would be one of the places where they could enjoy a great meal and fellowship.

I came from a farming family, but we didn't live on a farm. There were small farms all around our home, but our farm work took place about seven miles away on my grandparents' farm. My dad was a truck farmer. Lettuce, tomatoes, corn, peppers, broccoli, cauliflower, parsley, radishes, peas, beans and onions made for a colorful market stand. But the main crop raised each year was celery ... 13 acres of celery!

My dad was introduced to raising celery when he was the farm manager for another farmer in the area. In addition to the land on grandpa's farm, my dad rented some fields from a neighbor nearby. This was hard work and it was a family affair. Because I was the youngest of the family, I always got the jobs the older kids passed on.

When it was time to plant the small celery plants in the field, dad would drive the tractor and two of the older siblings would sit on the planter and feed the small celery plants into the rotating wheel that automatically placed the plant and a squirt of water into the ground. I got the job of walking along behind the planter and adjusting any of the plants that didn't get planted properly. I still remember the day brother Dan decided to mess with me and planted a whole row upside down! He was quite amused with the sight of all those plants with their roots sticking out of the ground. Dad finally heard my shouts of protest and corrected the wayward deeds of brother Dan.

Those days on the farm were interrupted every weekend when it was time to harvest the crops. We would take them into the preparation room in the barn, where they were trimmed and washed, placed in crates with ice sprinkled on top and loaded onto the truck in preparation for the Friday and Saturday market days in Reading, Pennsylvania, about 30 miles away. As we entered our early teens, mom and dad taught us how to interact with people and encourage them to purchase our scrumptious vegetables.

Those market days were long, leaving home around 4:30 in the morning and getting back in the early evening. The highlight of the day was stopping at Cloister Dairy for ice cream cones on the way home. Our family was raised on ice cream treats, so this stop was a natural and after a long day it broke up the trip home for dad, who would often get quite drowsy. My mom had a special alarm when she saw his eyes get heavy. Without warning she would scream at the top of her lungs bringing us all to attention.

Growing up in the country in the 1950s was much simpler than it is today. The backyards of the neighbors blended into each other with no need for fences and gates. One of my best friends, Carl, lived two doors away and they had a couple of ponies at the rear of their property. I was a bit jealous of him having those critters and proudly told him that we just bought a new pony, too. It didn't take long for his mom to ask my mom about our new pony. When she caught me in my story, I quickly searched for a way to rationalize my words by saying, "Well, I was talking about the new Pontiac that dad just bought. (Dad always pronounced it "pony-act"). She wasn't amused and I had to go and apologize. Perhaps that was the beginning of my enjoyment with the play on words. After all, a pun is its own "reword."

There was one time when I felt the need to correct the injustices done by the school bully. Knowing this kid walked home from school each day, I organized some of my buddies to collect walnuts from the trees along the road. When he walked by they unleashed their arsenal in his direction. Meanwhile, I took the bus home. As it turned out the "hit squad" shared my name with the principal and before long the Superintendent of Schools was requesting a meeting with my parents and me. That was an attention-getter for me and I realized that my actions, whether in deed or direction, had consequences.

When I was a junior in high school, there was a clothing drive for needy families. Students brought in used clothing and on the final day of collection, my homeroom teacher asked another student and me to carry the bags to the office before we took the bus home. Knowing we probably wouldn't catch the bus on time if we did that, Nick and I decided to let someone else do it. The next day our teacher made an example of us to the rest of the class. He assigned us to write a 500-word essay on "Why I Don't Like to Give to Others." (Considering all the used clothing we have given out over the years at Navajo Ministries, I wish I still had a copy of that essay).

The fact that I was the baby of the family, separated from my oldest brother, Bob, by 16 years, I didn't experience much sibling rivalry over the years. However, as the boys did some of their normal rough housing, they would occasionally step on my toys and break my new plastic trucks.

One of my favorite toys was a wooden duck that had a string attached. Dan and I were eight years apart. As he became a cool teenager, I would look for opportunities to bring him back to reality. Sometimes that meant telling mom and dad about questionable things I knew he was doing or saying. At times I would be brave enough to tell him off right to his face ... from a distance. One night I remember sharing one of my comments and he said, as he often did, "Come here and say that!" With my wooden duck hidden behind my back, I walked over to him. I repeated my words while whacking him on the head with the duck. Blood gushed from his head. I can still see mom running cold water over the cut in the kitchen sink. I thought he was going to die!

He didn't die, and I don't think he even needed stitches. The next morning my dad exhibited some tough love with me. He told me to get my favorite toy duck. We walked to the brush pile in the garden. He said, "Put the duck in the brush." He struck a match and the pile was in flames. As we watched it burn, he talked with me about the consequences of our choices. It was a life-lesson I never forgot.

My oldest brother, Bob, went off to the military following high school and spent some time in Alaska. I remember him saying he could see Russia from there. At Christmas I remember his black and white photo in his military uniform under the tree among the presents. We sorely missed him being with us at Christmas.

In the fall of 1954 my sister, Mary, still lived at home while her fiancé, Dave, was serving in Korea. Our part of the country took a direct hit from a powerful hurricane named Hazel. As the winds increased to 100 mph, I stood at the kitchen sink doing dishes with Mary when two big willow trees were toppled in our back yard. Mary screamed. I was amazed with the power of the wind that brought these huge trees crashing to the ground. The next morning I became an explorer, climbing up and through the broken limbs. A year later I would experience my own broken limb.

I was about 8 years old, and literally hanging around on a small Judas tree in the back yard. Brother Gene was mowing under the branch I was hanging onto with both hands. As he went by, he gave me a little push like you would do to someone on a swing. I fell to the ground. I went running into the house with my wrist hanging like a limp washcloth crying and shouting, "I broke my arm!" Mom was on the phone. Assuming that I was exaggerating, she lifted my wrist and I screamed with pain. This incident seemed like a simple childhood injury at the time. Later, it would prove to be a significant event that would change the course of my life.

Our family didn't enjoy traditional vacations. With the market stands open every Friday and Saturday, there wasn't much time to get away. But, Dad and Mom did try to get us to the Jersey Shore at least once each summer. We would leave early and have our picnic lunch on the beach. Sometimes our sandwiches were just that ... "sand"wiches. We would usually spend the night in a Tourist Home in Ocean City, which saved them some money. This town has a family atmosphere and to this day still has a ban on alcohol sales. It was a short break away from home, but provided us with great family memories. After a day of playing in the sand and surf, the boardwalk shops offered lots of great food including pizza by the slice, bars of fudge and caramel corn. As the tide came in, the waves would crash underneath the boardwalk. What a memorable break away from the farm work in Pennsylvania.

Another great family memory involved dad and my brothers. Every Monday night at 9 p.m. we "had a ball" with our church bowling league. We filled up eight lanes with 40 bowlers. While I averaged about 150 per game, some of these bowlers were averaging nearly 200! One of our Thanksgiving traditions included all of us guys heading to the bowling lanes to exercise away some of those extra calories that we consumed from mom's delicious turkey dinner, complete with shoo-fly pie.

I was fortunate to be born into a Christian family. Our church, First Church of God in Lancaster, was part of the Churches of God denomination headquartered in Findlay, Ohio. This beautiful, historic stone building with huge stain-glassed windows was the church home for families from all over the county. The basement was filled with Sunday school classes and the sanctuary upstairs could seat over 500 people, including the balcony located behind a huge maroon velvet curtain that was opened for special occasions.

We rarely missed going to church on Sundays, including Sunday evening services. Sunday in the Baker home began with devotions in the living room. Then we knelt for prayer before eating our hard-boiled eggs for breakfast. It was quite a tradition. In addition, I attended

Christian Endeavor meetings prior to the Sunday evening service.

It was during one of those Sunday evening services when, at 8 years of age, I realized that being in a Christian family wasn't enough. I needed to personally ask Jesus to come into my life. I remember our pastor, Rev. Joe Lewis, was speaking that evening prior to a week of revival meetings with a special speaker. When the invitation song was sung, that lump came into my throat again, reminding me that I needed to walk that aisle and commit my life to Christ. One of my friends, Bill Buckwalter, made his profession of faith that night also. It was February 17, 1957.

A few weeks later I had another spiritual highlight. I was baptized along with my dad, who had been sprinkled in a prior church, but now wanted to be immersed with me, his last-born son. We entered the waters at the front of the church together. I went under the water first, then stood to the back and watched dad do the same. My dad and I tended to be emotional and this was one of those times. Our tears, mixed with the dripping water from our heads, provided us with a night to remember. It was the beginning of a spiritual journey that would one day take me and my family across the country to Navajo Missions.

There were many faithful teachers and youth leaders in our church. They all impacted me in different ways. We didn't have a youth pastor, but these adults poured their lives into the children and youth for many years. Their investment produced several missionaries and pastors over the years. Little did I know then that Kay and I would be two of those God would call.

Every summer I attended VBS in one or two of the churches in the area. And, for one week I would attend church camp in Doubling Gap, about two hours from home in the mountains of Central Pennsylvania. This was a former hotel with three floors of bedrooms, a pool, huge lobby, cafeteria and wrap-around porch with a hundred wooden rockers. My sister and her husband Dave became superintendents of the camp in the late 1960s.

It was quite the place to be for a week in the summer and I enjoyed the break from all the farm work. When I was about 10, I remember the Bible class at camp taught by Rev. Forrest Weiss. He challenged us to think about missions. It was during that week that I began to think about one day becoming a missionary.

After high school graduation in the summer of 1965, I jumped at the opportunity to go on a foreign missions trip. Our church denomination was beginning mission work in Haiti. Teams were needed to go and help refurbish an existing compound and begin a church ministry to the Haitians living in the countryside about three hours outside of the capital city of Port-a-Prince. Our team of seven or eight men included our pastor.

This was an eye-opening experience. We were exposed to extreme poverty in a third-world country. In addition to the lack of daily food, we saw a spiritual hunger in the lives of the people, with many taking part in voodoo ceremonies. In the midst of their sad existence, their faces lit up with joy when they came for the evening church services. Today, that mission work is thriving. The Churches of God in Haiti includes 33 churches and mission stations with over 6,000 members.

For me, those two weeks in Haiti watered the seed of missions that was planted in my spirit several years earlier at church camp. I couldn't help but remember Paul's words to the Corinthians, "So neither he who plants nor he who waters is anything, but only God, who makes things grow." (I Corinthians 3:7)

As I moved through my teen years, school, farm work and church youth group kept me busy. I also began to help my brother Gene on Saturdays. He was a successful door-to- door Fuller Brush Man. Saturdays he delivered the orders that he sold the week before. I realized I enjoyed interacting with the people in the homes when delivering the products. I loved being around people, which was one of the reasons I was thinking about becoming a barber after high school.

Gene was also serving as the youth leader for the young people at our church. He asked me if I had noticed Kay Duing, who was two years younger than me. Her family were also long-time members of the church. At that time I wasn't dating anyone and hadn't given her much thought.

My first car was a 1956 four-door Buick that I bought for $660 before I turned 16. After I got my license, I became one of the drivers to take kids home after youth group outings. Kay was the girl who eventually made her way from the back seat, dropped off first, to the front seat, dropped off last. I definitely had now taken notice of her, and I liked what I saw.

Chapter Three

GROWING UP COUNTRY

I n the quietness of early fall mornings in Lancaster
County, my father would come into my room and
gently awaken me. "It's time to get up," he would say.
Darkness still filled the room, and my bed would feel
toasty warm. But even the warmth of the covers couldn't
keep me in bed those mornings. It was another Saturday.
It was my own special time alone with Dad.

My dad was an avid hunter and angler. Every fall,
Dad and I would spend our Saturday mornings driving
to York County, Pennsylvania, where my dad's uncle and
aunt, Roy and Hilda Lausch, had a farm. On our way,
we would often stop for breakfast at a little diner called
Nellie's. I would sit proudly beside Dad, feeling all the
joy that comes with being Daddy's little girl. Finishing the
hour drive, we would arrive at Uncle Roy's farm. There my
dad and his uncle would walk through the fields hunting
for pheasants or rabbits and I would spend the day with
Aunt Hilda. Gathering eggs from the chickens, feeding
the cats, exploring the barnyard and helping her in the

large farmhouse kitchen made the hours go by quickly. These times at Uncle Roy's farm fed my love for animals and the outdoors.

Late afternoon, my dad and I would return home. It was usually a quiet ride as I dozed most of the way home. I found great comfort, protection and security in the presence of my father. I know today my relationship with Dad was a catalyst for me to begin a relationship with my heavenly Father that would sustain me through a lifetime.

My family consisted of my father and mother and two siblings. My parents Parke and Ruth (Brooks) Duing were married on May 3, 1943. On September 2, 1945 my sister Donna Lou was born. Three and a half years later, on May 6, 1949, I came into the world, followed by my brother, Parke Jr., born August 23, 1953. When I was about 4 years old, we moved to my mother's childhood home in the country. The two-story home was built by my grandfather, Amos Brooks. It was one of seven homes on a country road. All our neighbors were older, which meant Donna, Parke and I were the only children in the neighborhood. It was a safe, loving environment to grow up in, as neighbors on both sides of our home encouraged our visits and loved on us as their own grandchildren.

My dad was a farmer at heart, so we had our share of chickens, rabbits, dogs and cats. One day, much to my mother's dismay, he brought home three sheep, hoping they would eat the grass in our large backyard and lessen the need for mowing. Cherry trees grew in this area and the sheep seemed to enjoy standing on their back legs to reach the leaves of the trees more than eating the grass. After several occasions when the sheep jumped the fence and ran through the neighbors' property, my mother put an end to Dad's sheep raising. As an adult now, I can understand her frustration and embarrassment when the sheep would escape, but as a child, I was really sad when they had to find a new home.

One Easter, my dad brought home two colored chicks for my sister and me. In those days, you could purchase chicks that were dyed in colors of pink, blue, green or yellow. Having the limited creativity of young children, we named the chicks Happy and Easter. I thought my chick was wonderful and fed and watered him faithfully as he lived in a cardboard box in our kitchen.

My sister wasn't as enthusiastic, and as a result, her chick, Happy, died within a few days. Easter flourished and soon had to move to the chicken house with the other chickens. He was a wonderful pet and grew into a feisty, red rooster that ruled the henhouse. Combining my love of animals with my second love, reading, I would spend time in the chicken house, sitting on an up-side-down peach basket, reading to my beloved rooster. Life was sometimes lonely in the country and, despite the teasing from my siblings, I enjoyed the company of Easter and my other animal friends.

My mother's parents, Amos and Mary Brooks, separated when I was very young. My grandmother remained in the family home and a short time later, my parents bought the home and my grandmother continued to live with us. She would often care for my cousins, too, spending a portion of the week in their homes. Grandma was heavy set with warm "fluffy" arms that welcomed us onto her lap whenever we needed a hug. Sitting in her bedroom on occasional mornings, with the smell of Bengay ever-present, I would watch her brush her long, gray, untrimmed hair and twist it into a bun on the back of her head. Being of Mennonite background, she would *affix a netted covering, which later she wore only for church services.*

My parents had a strong work ethic, passed down to all three of their children. After serving in the Army, my father began working for the post office. In 1953 he was offered a position with Lancaster Photo Engraving. Eventually, this led to involvement in the offset printing business, resulting in the opportunity to set up a complimentary business to Lancaster Photo Engraving in the same building, which became known as Parke E. Duing Lithographic Plates. My brother joined the business after he graduated from college and continued the business after Dad retired in 1986. My brother continues this business to this day.

Being a small business, it was often necessary for my mother to work in the shop. She took care of billing customers, answering phones, running deliveries, etc. During those times, my grandmother would care for us at home. There were winter days of heavy snow when our road would not see a snowplow before it was time for Dad to leave for work. He would don his boots and heavy winter jacket and start in the direction of the shop, until he would get picked up by a customer with a four-wheel drive, who would take him the rest of the way to work. Snow was no excuse for not getting to work and I cannot remember my dad ever taking a sick day.

Our home was near a railroad track and it was common for men to walk the tracks and eventually hop a train. We would sometimes have a "hobo" come to our door and ask for something to eat. My mother was always gracious in feeding them and showed us in many ways her gift of hospitality. She always had a cup of tea or coffee for any neighbor who stopped by for a visit. In addition to the bread man and the milk man who stopped by weekly with deliveries, these visitors added variety to our days. We spent evenings outdoors until the sun went down. My brother and I especially enjoyed playing outdoors and sometimes working alongside Dad and Mom in the large garden. There was always mowing to do with a push mower, or some other type of outdoor work we could put our hands to as a family. If we worked especially hard, Mom or Dad would suggest an evening drive and we would all jump into the car. We kids would watch for the particular roads Dad would take, hoping for just the right turns and bends that would lead us to an Amish farm where they made homemade ice cream. What a delight to walk into their old barn and pick out our favorite ice cream flavor. We did not mind the fact there were flies everywhere and the smell of manure, or that our "servers" were barefooted. It was a special treat and we loved it.

Our cousins played a major part in our childhood. We often spent time in one another's homes, playing games, learning crafts, jumping rope and, due to the popularity of "The Lone Ranger," playing cowboys and Indians. My cousin, Dale, two years younger than me, and always the cowboy, was usually successful in catching me and tying me to a tree. Thankfully, his yard was not that big, and my grandmother or aunt would see me from the kitchen window and come to my rescue if he went off to another play activity and forgot me.

One day, while my mother was giving my aunt a perm, Dale and I were playing hide and seek in my house. Our attic was a fun place to explore and my mother kept plastic garment bags filled with winter clothes hung on the attic rafters. I'm not sure whose idea it was, but it was decided I would climb into the plastic garment bag and

Dale would pretend he couldn't find me. Then he would enlist our moms to come and look for me. After I climbed into the bag, Dale zipped it to the top and began his pretend "search." Because of his nature to get sidetracked, Dale forgot about me until one of our mothers asked where I was. I can only imagine the horror my mother experienced when Dale took her to the garment bag and she found me passed out in the bottom of the bag. That was my only near-death experience and one my cousin and I would laugh about in the years to come.

My father's brother and wife, Charles and Sarah Duing, had a daughter born to them six weeks after I was born. As elementary-aged children, Cindy and I were inseparable. Friday nights would often find me spending the night at Cindy's house. Cindy and her parents lived in an upstairs apartment over a small general store. My paternal grandmother, Dora Duing, lived in the adjacent apartment and we enjoyed the freedom of going back and forth to grandma Duing's home whenever I was visiting Cindy.

Cindy had some physical challenges that made our bond even stronger. Being an only child, Cindy craved the time we spent together. Our relationship also taught me compassion and stirred within me the desire to help those with special needs in a tangible way. I am grateful for the way God allowed my relationship with Cindy to teach me empathy and the value of serving others.

Fear and worry were constant companions as I attended elementary and junior high school. My earliest memories of first grade included a little friend named Stevie. It was a common occurrence for our teacher to tie Stevie to his desk chair or smack his fingers with a ruler. He often missed recess because he couldn't complete the work we were given. Although I never personally experienced mistreatment in the classroom, fear set in during those early days of what "might happen" if I did something wrong.

Headaches and stomach aches were daily occurrences and by third grade, I was making daily visits to the nurse's office. Mrs. Sharfenburger would allow me to rest for a few minutes, give me a hug and send me back to class. Her daily presence and reassuring words would get me through my years of elementary school.

Junior high brought a new school, new friends, new challenges and new fears. I hated going to seven different classes and having to learn to adjust to seven different teachers, each having their own way of doing things. I had a strong desire to please each one and do all they required in hopes of receiving good grades. Fear often blocked my ability to concentrate and learn, sometimes making it difficult to remember instructions or homework given.

I had a terrible fear of my first male teacher. He was a stern, bottom-line type of man who expected us to grasp his teachings without repetition. One day he was lecturing my class and walking up and down the aisles. My purse had slipped out from under my desk and he tripped on it as he came up the aisle. He picked up my purse and carried it to the front of the room, changing the theme of his lecture to the size of purses and the many unnecessary items we girls carried in them. He then proceeded to dump the contents of my purse on his desk and show how many items were unnecessary for me to have in my purse that day.

The humiliation from that experience only confirmed my distorted view of school as an unsafe place. It also made me confront the truth of my relationship with Jesus. Either He was my Savior and friend, who promised to walk with me through every circumstance of life, or He was just a good person who promised nice things, but was unable to really make any difference in my life. It was a life-changing experience to begin walking in the knowledge of His presence with me every moment of every day. When fear threatened to consume me, I would place my hand at my side and imagine Christ holding my hand and walking with me to the next class. Slowly, my fears began to subside as I allowed Jesus' presence to fill me with His peace.

It was also during this time my sister, Donna, experienced two separate occasions when she was unable to walk. Each time, a couple weeks would pass with her being in the hospital, unable to put weight on her legs. Tests would be run, but they were always inconclusive. Just as quickly as her legs would buckle underneath her and she would be unable to walk, she would later gain strength and begin walking again. These were difficult days for our family. The unknown is always so scary and doctors could not make any prediction concerning Donna's future and whether there would be more reoccurrences of her inability to walk. As a young teenage girl, Donna faced these experiences with determination and faith.

By the time I was in 10th grade, Jim and I began building a friendship with each other. Several young people in our youth group had begun relationships and as a result, we did a lot of our dating with other couples. We built strong friendships that continued long into our adult years. Even today, many of these friends bless our lives and welcome us "home" whenever we are in Pennsylvania.

The summer before I entered my senior year, it was necessary for my parents to sell our home. High Welding Steel Co. was buying the properties on our road in order to expand their business. The timing was right for my parents to sell our property, but it meant a change in school districts for me and for my brother, who was entering junior high. The old fears that had been ever-present during my elementary and junior high years began to torment me as I thought about a new school, new friends and new teachers.

I remember one night, as our move was approaching and I was facing the possibility of my senior year in a new school, my father came to my room and sat on the edge of my bed. In his confident way, he told me, "Kate, I don't want you worrying about going to a new school. Your mother and I will work something out for you to finish your schooling at Conestoga Valley." When he left the room, I didn't have a clue how I would be able to start my senior year in another month at my same school. But Dad had said he would take care of it and that was enough for me. Peace settled in my heart and by the time school started, my dad had arranged with the school to pay tuition for me to complete my senior year at Conestoga Valley. It would be many years later until I was able to fully appreciate the sacrifice my parents made to not only pay my tuition, but to transport me back and forth to school every day for a whole year.

The rest of my social life consisted of church and activities with my friends from Sunday School, Junior Church and later, Youth Group. My parents were members of the Lancaster First Church of God and our family *was usually there whenever the doors were open. Being born and raised in Lancaster County, which consisted of 16 school districts, my friends came from a variety of schools. We were rivals when it came to football games, but united in our love for the Lord and the awesome people who taught us of His love as we grew up in the church. As an elementary-aged child, I responded to an altar call during a week of evangelistic services and gave my heart and life to Jesus.*

Today, many of our churches have paid youth leaders, children's workers, etc., but that wasn't the case when I was a child. But we did have the consistency of faithful followers of the Lord who loved children and young people and devoted their lives to teaching us what it meant to follow Christ. Two couples from church who added to the spiritual instruction I regularly received at home, were Ken and Vivian Warfel and Elvin and Gladys Neff. The Warfels served over 13 years as leaders in our young people's group on Sunday evenings. They were loving and nurturing, making each one of us feel valued for who we were. They provided fun times of teenage fellowship, allowing all of us to grow socially, as well as spiritually.

The Neffs directed our Junior Church program every Sunday morning for all of my childhood years while the adults were in Sunday morning service. Here we learned the joy of Jesus by singing songs, learning Bible principles and making crafts. We also learned this dedicated couple had a love for all of us kids that endeared them to Jim and me long into our adult years. Their faithfulness even extended into the lives of our own children, who attended Junior Church when we would visit family in Pennsylvania during our earliest years of living at

Navajo Missions. Gladys also faithfully taught Sunday School for 50 years.

Two other people who greatly influenced my life were William and Pauline Malehorn. After serving as missionaries in Farmington, New Mexico at a boarding school for Navajo students, William and Pauline retired and moved to the community of Neffsville, Pennsylvania. They attended our church and often shared their memories and experiences of living on the mission field. As a child, I can remember Pauline dressing in a traditional Navajo skirt and blouse and sharing her love for the Navajo (The Diné) and the joy she had in teaching the children who attended the school where she and William taught. It was through her sharing in church services that seeds of love were planted in my heart for the Navajo people. I never dreamed I would one day be living less than a mile from the school where Pauline and her husband taught Navajo students for so many years.

While I did not have many close friends in school, it was during these years of regular church attendance that Christian friends with similar values surrounded me. It was there where I found acceptance, love, and Godly direction for my life. It was there I learned my life without a relationship with Jesus would lead to emptiness and hopelessness. It was also there in that youth group I found the love of my life – Jim Baker.

Chapter Four

TWO BECOME ONE

I will never forget that day in my sophomore year at Hempfield High School. It was November 22, 1963 when the announcement came over the loudspeaker as I sat in Study Hall in the Music classroom. "President Kennedy was shot in Dallas!" Before long we got the rest of the story and heard that he indeed had died of an assassin's bullet. That was the beginning of non-stop TV news coverage of the unfolding story. I still remember coming home from church on that following Sunday and turning on our console black and white TV just as Jack Ruby fired his gun in that parking garage, taking the life of Lee Harvey Oswald.

The world as we knew it was becoming a frightening place to live. The Cold War with Russia was intensifying. Vietnam was drawing America into a war against communism that many viewed as having no way to win. United States leaders lost the American public's support for the war. Protests swept across the nation. And, the tie-dyed hippie subculture began its development as a youth movement in the country, complete with free love and psychedelic rock concerts.

Prophesy preachers were predicting the end of the earth and the Second Coming of Christ could happen at any moment. As a young person raised in the conservative "Bible Belt" area of Lancaster County, Pennsylvania, I had no interest in crawling into a Hippie Volkswagen bus and heading out to a protest march. But, I was concerned about the Vietnam War that was looming in my future. The mandatory draft was taking graduating seniors into the armed forces to fight in the jungles of Vietnam.

While there were a number of conscientious objectors in our county, including the Mennonites and Amish, that would not be a reason for me to not serve my country. There were also exemptions for those married with children, those attending college or health reasons. Since my future plans were to become a barber, that training would not be considered as a student deferment.

It would not be until the middle of my junior year that I would be surprised with the results of a routine school physical examination. It was then the nurse alerted me to the fact that I had severe scoliosis of the spine. She advised my parents to have me seen by a doctor and possibly an orthopedic specialist to determine what should be done. After several visits to doctors it was suggested that I might need corrective surgery in the future, but for the time being, I should "wait and see."

In the meantime I began having appointments with a chiropractor. It was interesting to note that after my first chiropractic exam he wondered if I had any kind of fall or accident when I was 8 to 10 years old. I immediately thought back to my fall from the tree limb when I was that age. While we thought the broken wrist was the only injury I sustained, my chiropractor believed that fall was a factor in initiating the scoliosis during those crucial growth years that followed. This childhood injury now was an instrumental event that would prevent me from serving in Vietnam. I walked out with a 4-F rating, (Not Qualified for Military Service due to medical reasons).

As I moved toward high school graduation I remained active in our church youth group and became more interested in one of the girls, Kay Duing. Our first official date was April 23, 1965 when I took her to *"Oklahoma,"* not the state, but the operetta put on by my high school. It was the beginning of a relationship that developed over the next four years that led to our marriage on April 19, 1969.

After graduation I continued to pursue the possibility of beginning Barber School in Harrisburg. I filled out the paper work, which included scholarship assistances and sent it in. When I showed up for that first day of classes on a rainy Monday morning, I quickly realized that they didn't have my application for some reason. I would have to resubmit the paperwork and delay my commencement of classes.

As I turned around and drove back to Lancaster, there was a stirring within my spirit that God had other plans for me. By the end of the day I found myself with a full-time job at a local printing company that my Uncle Earl, a draftsman, told me about. And, my brother Gene, a Fuller Brush salesman, also told me there was an opening for another salesman in the county. I took that job on a part-time basis and after six months realized I was making more money in that part-time job than I was with the full-time position at the print shop.

I quit the printing job and went full-time with the door-to-door sales position. That job would provide me with fun, friends and funds as I knocked on the doors of our community selling mops, brushes, cleaning supplies along with a catalogue of many other items. The "traditional uniform" for this profession included a tie and jacket and raincoat or umbrella for the rainy days. Anyone younger than 35 most likely has never met a Fuller Brush Man, nor know much about him. The Fuller Brush Man belongs to your mother's and grandmother's generations, a time when stay-at-home moms were the norm. Those were the days when somebody would actually answer the door without worrying about a stranger being there. For the first 50 years of its existence, beginning in 1906, the Fuller Brush sales force called on nearly 9 out of 10 American homes.

There were several Fuller Brush salesmen in Lancaster County at that time. Elvin Neff, a long-time member of our church, along with my brother, Gene, and I were consistently ranked in the top 10 of the Mid-Atlantic sales force. This was a profession that included some famous Americans such as Dick Clark, Dennis Quaid and Rev. Billy Graham.

I had many fascinating experiences during my 10 years as a door-to-door salesman, as well as many lessons about life and the human nature. I learned to persist and persevere after realizing that only one of every 10 doors knocked on would produce a sale. And, I learned to not have many sick days when working on a straight commission basis. I also discovered that if I first developed a relationship with the customer, my products would more easily sell themselves. As a Christian this occupation provided many opportunities to share my faith, provide encouragement and pray for those who had needs.

Little did I know then that one day I would be doing just that 2,000 miles away in a place known as Navajoland.

For three years, Jim and I dated each other. Being two years older than me, he began working while I finished high school and then attended McCann's Business School in Reading, Pennsylvania. Reading was an hour's drive from Lancaster and Jim would take me to Reading every Sunday evening where I would stay for a week of classes. I lived in the Berkshire Hotel, where the third floor rooms were rented through the YWCA. Many female students who attended McCanns lived there and it was a safe environment.

My roommate, Sally, became my best friend. She had started school earlier than I did, so she willingly familiarized me with the layout of the school, where certain classes were held, and introduced me to other students. We shared our evening meals together at local restaurants and spent evenings doing homework. Usually being short on cash by Thursday nights, we would pick up a pizza at a local pizzeria and bring it back to our room to eat. Any leftover pizza was placed on the old hot water heating radiator and eaten for breakfast the next morning. Sally completed her classes and moved back home several months before I graduated.

Because I was only an hour away, I went home every Friday night for the weekend. Jim's parents worked at a market in Reading every Friday. I would walk the 10 blocks to the market after my last Friday class, eat some supper and ride home with them to Lancaster. During these drives, I got to know Jim's parents better and fell in love with his dad's sense of humor. It was easy to see where Jim got his appreciation for good jokes and puns, which was one of the things that had drawn me to him. My dad always had a fun sense of humor and I had always enjoyed hearing him laugh and joke around with his friends. Being around these three men who loved to laugh helped me to take life less seriously.

After three years of dating, I finally got up the courage to ask Kay's dad for her hand in marriage. That was back in the days when her dad still smoked. He had just lit up one of his cigars when I popped the question. As he blew the smoke in my direction he jokingly said, "Well, just remember, boy ... she doesn't come with any money!" Through my choking and coughing from the smoke, I made sure he knew that was fine with me. On April 27, 1968 I took Kay to eat at a nice restaurant at the Overlook Golf Course. Before we got out of the car I pulled a box of photo slides out of the glove compartment. An avid photographer, I was always showing her my latest "developments." This particular box held a real gem ... a diamond engagement ring. She said "Yes!"

My parents didn't want me getting married until I graduated from business school, so I was highly motivated to complete my classes. Most of the classes were self-paced, so the harder you worked, the quicker you could complete the courses. I began my classes as soon as I graduated from high school and within 16 months I had completed a two-year course. With diploma in hand, I returned home and began looking for a job and preparing for a wedding. A former Sunday School teacher, Earl Givler, knew I was looking for a job. He told me about an opening for a secretary at the office of the Superintendent of Schools for Lancaster County. I was hired and loved my job working in this office.

As we prepared for our Spring wedding, Jim continued to set aside any extra funds to be used for our home when we got married. He was actually able to save up enough money so we could provide a down payment on the construction of a new house in Willow Street, Pennsylvania. April 19, 1969, Jim and I were married. I can still remember the thrill of driving away from the reception and heading for our two week honeymoon to Florida. After four years of dating, curfews and never enough time together, we were finally able to start life together on our own. After returning from our honeymoon, we took up residence in a small apartment just two doors away from Jim's childhood home. The remodeled upper level of this former pony barn was quite adequate as we began our married life together awaiting our new house to be completed.

Vo-tech schools were beginning to open in Lancaster County and one of the men in my office, Richard Murr, was transferring to Willow Street Vo-tech school as a guidance counselor. The school was only a couple miles from the home we were building. I applied for the secretarial position for the guidance counselor and was accepted. I worked for Mr. Murr until our first child was born two years later.

A few months after our wedding, I was driving from the countryside south of Willow Street, which would soon become our home town. As I entered the town limits I began to slow to the village speed limit. I noticed an elementary-aged boy on his bicycle on the right just ahead at an intersection. As I approached the intersection he rode his bike right into the path of my car. I hit the brakes but it wasn't enough to avert hitting him. The impact was enough to knock him to the cement highway causing him to hit his head on the pavement.

Within just a few moments his mother was next to her son, who was unconscious. I still remember her screams, some of which were directed toward me. I was horrified at the scene before me as I saw bright red blood coming from his mouth. Before long the ambulance was on the scene and he was rushed off to the Lancaster hospital. Later I heard that they had to revive him twice on the way to the hospital.

The accident happened around lunch time, but my day was over. I felt a heaviness in my heart that I had never experienced before. That evening Kay and I went to the hospital to see how this young boy was doing. As I recall he was in a coma at the time. We waited in the hallway so we could visit with his parents. I expressed my grief over the accident and they were glad I was there to show support for their family.

As it turned out, what I thought was blood coming from the boy's mouth was actually from strawberries that he had eaten for lunch. The head injuries were severe enough, however, that he lost his hearing in one ear and missed a year of school. A couple of days after the accident the police reports were finalized showing that the skid marks revealed I was driving within the reduced speed limit entering the town. To this day, my eyes are always wary of children on bicycles near the roadway.

Toward the end of summer we were able to move into our new house, less than a mile from the site of the accident. After living in a tiny apartment we loved the spaciousness of our new home. It was a three-bedroom split-foyer house located in the southern part of Lancaster County. The rolling hills of the area made for a picturesque place for us to begin our lives together, looking forward to one day starting our family. The name of our street was appropriate – Pleasant View Drive.

For as long as I can remember, I wanted to be a mother. We wanted to be sure we could live on Jim's income, so I could stay home when we started our family. A little over two years later we were blessed with the arrival of our first born, Lisa Karen Baker, on October 27, 1971. Motherhood was all that I had expected it would be. I loved caring for Lisa and preparing for Jim's arrival at home for supper each evening.

Surrounded by loving family, a good job, a wonderful church, we were content with life. But then, God started to mess with us.

Chapter Five

"SNARED" INTO MINISTRY

As a young married couple we continued to work with the young people of our church. I even got a guitar and started picking my way through some of the popular choruses. In the late sixties, the youth group was known as Christian Endeavor. Then the name changed to reflect our Church name ... Churches of God Youth Advance or C.G.Y.A. Many times our youth group would join other churches in our denomination for rallies and special events. Kay and I really enjoyed interacting with the kids.

Denny and Cindy Andrew were good friends from our church, having grown up together. They got married just a few months after Kay and I in the same beautiful sanctuary of the First Church of God. We had much in common with them, including a passion for sharing Christ's love with the lost.

While Denny was finishing seminary at Findlay College in Ohio, we called them to let them know Kay and I were expecting our first child. After a "pregnant pause" they giggled and said, "We were just going to call you guys to tell you that we are pregnant!" As it turned out we went into separate hospitals in Lancaster on the same day to await the arrival of our babies. Cindy delivered a baby girl, Amy, late in the night of October 26th and Kay delivered Lisa a few hours later in the early hours of October 27th.

By now, Denny had completed seminary in Findlay and he and Cindy had relocated back to Lancaster. Denny and I got quite bold in our witnessing in 1973 when the movie *"The Exorcist"* came out in the theatres. This was the story of a 12-year-old girl who was demon possessed. A priest recognizes the necessity for a show-down with an old demonic enemy. A graphic scene of exorcism made this a very controversial film for that day. We printed up tracts, "What About Exorcism?" and enlisted volunteers to help hand them out to movie goers at the end of each showing. The tract shared crucial verses from the Bible that explained the power of God and how He can deliver people from their sins.

I grew up listening to WDAC Christian radio. It went on the air in 1959 and was the first FM station in the Lancaster area providing commercial programming at a time when virtually no car radios and few table radios had an FM band. As I became a young adult in the 1970s, Denny (who was now a pastor in the area) and I began toying with the idea of starting another Christian station that would feature more contemporary music and reach the younger generation of listeners. We soon realized that we didn't have the resources to make that happen. (It is interesting to note, in 1984, a Contemporary Christian station went on the air in Lancaster and continues to reach the younger generation of listeners).

In the early seventies, the Jesus Movement began to move across the country from its roots at Calvary Chapel in California. These free-spirited beach lovers were accustomed to the fun and flash of entertainment, and the Maranatha Music Nights provided an excellent form of Christian entertainment.

But for young people in other parts of the country, there were often no churches such as Calvary Chapel (churches that opened their doors to barefooted, blue-jeaned teens who needed acceptance). The festivals became church for many young people—outdoor sanctuaries with the sky as a canopy. For many people, the Jesus festivals marked the beginning of new lives in Christ.

In August 1973, a central Pennsylvania potato field became one of those sanctuaries. Mennonite Harold Zimmerman organized Jesus '73, the start of an annual tradition. Jesus '73 featured three days of festival, with guest appearances by top-name Christian musicians and speakers. Young people and adults of all faiths attended Jesus '73. Kay and I, along with her sister Donna and her husband Dick, attended that first festival and really enjoyed the atmosphere of praise and worship that filled the hillside and lifted us from our church traditions.

The breaking down of denominational barriers had already become a trait of the Jesus people. Baptists worshipped with Assembly of God members; Catholics fellowshipped with Mennonites. Musicians from the Church of the Nazarene played in Presbyterian churches, gospel performers from the Church of God in Christ sang with Methodists. In the midst of them all, there were a large number of non-Christians who heard the gospel and responded to it. This coming together of the people of faith was refreshing. Little did I know then that one day

God would use me to bring people of faith together in the Four Corners region of our country.

In the fall of 1973 our home church decided to do something different from the traditional fall revival services where a guest pastor would come to speak for four nights. I was on the church council at that time and we heard about Lay Witness Missions that churches were having for a weekend. These Lay Witness Missions began in a Methodist prayer cell a few years earlier.

After much planning and preparation, nearly 50 men and women arrived on a Friday night, which not surprisingly began with a potluck supper. The evening program included praise and worship, and some of the team shared what God was doing in their lives. I think the most impactful part of the weekend for me was learning these people were all lay people from many backgrounds, just sharing how much Jesus had done in their lives.

Saturday included men getting together with men and women having tea gatherings in their homes. The youth had separate events throughout the weekend, too. Many of these times included small group settings. Our church friends were sharing needs and hopes and dreams that had never been shared before. Saturday night our beautiful sanctuary, with breathtaking stained glass windows, was dimly lit as we entered. More dramatic testimonies were shared ending with dozens of our members at the altar, many in tears praying and seeking God for a closer, more intimate relationship with Him.

Sunday morning the team members led our Sunday School class discussions and shared in the church service. That evening the team had departed and just our members came together to share our experiences of the weekend. There were more tears as our friends shared what God had done in their lives and how His presence was more real than ever before. Many were humbled as they saw God move in the hearts of those who perhaps kept their faith to themselves, but were now boldly revealing the moving of the Holy Spirit in their lives.

One of our elders was a successful accountant in our area. He stood up and shared how God had convicted him to stop smoking and believed that he was possibly being called into the mission field. After a couple of years of ministry training he and his wife moved to Bangladesh and served there for several years.

Then, there was us ... Jim and Kay Baker. God was stirring within our spirits through this weekend, too. Tears flooded our eyes at times as we sensed his presence in a new way. Could it be that He would have a plan for our lives that would move us out of our comfort zone in Lancaster County?

Within a few weeks we were joining others from our church and becoming involved in teams going to other Lay Witness weekends in the area. We focused our ministry and outreach to the young people in the churches we visited. We were refreshed in our spirits as we shared our testimonies and God's love with people we had never met. As we saw God use our lives to touch others, we began to realize that He was grabbing our attention, preparing us for something special. We didn't know what it would look like, but we knew that when the time was right, He would reveal His divine plan to us.

Life took on a happy rhythm as we began enjoying parenthood. Jim's days were spent selling door to door. My days were filled with mothering Lisa. We lived near a park, so daily walks were part of our day. Lisa would push her baby stroller to the park. A couple times a week we would go for an evening drive with Jim and sit in the car and read books together while Jim delivered Fuller Brush orders. It wasn't long until we began thinking of another child.

We had planned for our first child after I had worked our first two years of marriage. No sooner had we begun talking about a baby, Lisa was conceived. We expected the same thing when we planned for baby number 2, and within a short time, I was pregnant again. Everything we planned seemed to fall into place and life held the joy of dreams fulfilled.

At the time, we had no way of knowing God would use the life of this new baby to change our world. We had driven several hours to participate in a Lay Witness Mission in Maryland. By now, we had begun leading the youth during these weekends. By the time we reached the home we were to stay in for the weekend, I had begun feeling ill and bleeding. After a visit to the emergency room, I remained in bed for the weekend. Arriving home, we visited with my doctor and I was put on bed rest. Only three months along in my pregnancy, things were not looking very good.

A couple weeks later, I lost the baby we had already come to love. For the first time in our married lives, our life hit an unexpected bump in the road. We were forced to look at our lives and determine who was to be in charge of our future. Were we going to continue to make our plans and ask God to bless them? Or were we going to depend on God to make His will known to us and give us direction and a plan for our future? It wasn't a hard decision to make. God had gotten our attention, and as we grieved for our baby, we also began seeking His will for our lives, whatever that would be.

On the last Sunday evening of each month our church had a Missions service held in the fellowship hall on the lower level of this beautiful stone building. Being a very mission-minded church, Rhoda Kauffman, Mary Hershey, Evelyn Shuey and Lois Habecker were veteran missionaries whom our church supported as they served in India, Pakistan and Bangladesh. Kay and I always admired their service and commitment to the Lord as they served in these destitute countries of the world.

It was at one of those Mission services, in September 1974, when a pastor from our denomination, Jim Snare, came to share his stories and show slides from his family's visit to Navajoland in the early 1970s. They had spent a couple of weeks at Navajo Missions in Farmington while they were there. After the Snares' visit with Jack Drake, the founder of Navajo Missions, they invited him to come to Central Pennsylvania, where they lined him up for numerous speaking engagements. After those meetings Pastor Jim asked Jack to leave his slides and literature with him and he would tell Jack's stories and share the work of the mission to anyone who was interested.

Our 3-year-old daughter Lisa was ill that day, so Kay stayed home with her and I attended the evening service. This was a divine appointment. While many in the service enjoyed hearing the stories about the Navajo and their needs, I began to sense the moving of the Holy Spirit in my life. This was not just another mission service. This became a *calling* to mission service to some of our "first Americans," the Navajo.

At the close of the service I spent some time talking with the Snares and snatched up one of each of the literature pieces that were on the table. I could hardly wait to get home and tell Kay about what I experienced at church that evening. We laid out all the literature and looked closely at the photos and read every word. Those Navajo Trails newsprint publications showed lots of stories about the ministry houseparents had with Navajo boys and girls who lived in the mission homes.

Could it be that God was showing us a place to serve that would involve children? Could it be that God in His sense of humor would use a pastor named Snare to lead us into ministry? (One of Webster's definitions for snare is "anything dangerous, etc. that tempts or attracts"). We were definitely being attracted to do something that could also be quite dangerous, knowing that Satan would not like the idea of us moving 2,000 miles away to begin full-time service to God.

Chapter Six

THE CALL

I t was hard to sleep the night we heard about Navajo Missions. The next morning I began to second guess the stirring we felt the night before. I thought, "Surely other people get similar feelings from a presentation and then they go on with life as they know it and perhaps add a ministry to their prayer list or maybe even give an extra donation to help their mission work." Then, I could almost hear the Holy Spirit say, "Nice try, Jim. You're not getting off that easy."

Over the next few days the Navajo Missions' literature was put inside our dresser drawer. Maybe if we didn't see the faces of those dear Navajo children, we would go about our comfortable lifestyle in Pennsylvania. But, we opened that drawer and looked at those faces every day. After praying and discussing these feelings, Kay and I agreed that we would just write a letter to our denomination headquarters in Findlay, Ohio and see if they had any plans to someday start a work among the Navajos. They communicated back to us saying they were interested in beginning a work among the Navajo, but at this time they had no connections. So, now we were back to the connection to Navajo Missions that was made through the Snares on that Sunday night in September.

What was God saying to us? I asked Him for a specific scripture that would clearly show us what He was up to. As I was eating some lunch in my car that sunny day, I looked up at a series of telephone poles and wires and this scripture reference seemed to appear among the wires ... II Timothy 2: 1-7. While I'm not one who sees visions, God knew He needed to speak to me visually. He decided to "wire me" His message.

I quickly got out my pocket-sized New Testament in the Living Bible translation to see what those verses said. *"Timothy, my dear son, be strong with the special favor God gives you in Christ Jesus. You have heard me teach many things that have been confirmed by many reliable witnesses. Teach these great truths to trustworthy people who are able to pass them on to others. Endure suffering along with me, as a good soldier of Christ Jesus. And as Christ's soldier, do not let yourself become tied up in the affairs of this life, for then you cannot satisfy the one who has enlisted you in his army. Follow the Lord's rules for doing his work, just as an athlete either follows the rules or is disqualified and wins no prize. Hardworking farmers are the first to enjoy the fruit of their labor. Think about what I am saying. The Lord will give you understanding in all these things."*

These verses spoke directly to my heart reminding me of what God had done for me and now it was time to pass His message on to others. And, I was also cautioned to not hold on to the "comfort zone" of living in Pennsylvania with family and friends. I was reminded that if I was going to be like a soldier, an athlete or a good farmer, I would need to follow His direction and He would give us understanding in His call.

The next Sunday our pastor's sermon was about Jesus walking on the water and Peter's decision to step out of the boat and follow Him. Okay, now we couldn't just ignore the voice of God. Kay and I decided to fast and pray on Monday. At this point in time we hadn't related to our family what God was doing in our lives. We wanted to hear from Him and didn't want to be distracted with lots of other voices, even from family members. Finally, on Tuesday morning I was knocking on doors for my Fuller Brush job, several miles from home. God impressed me to look at Galatians 6:9. *"So don't get tired of doing what is good. Don't get discouraged and give up, for we will reap a harvest of blessing at the appropriate time."* (LB) I said, "Okay God, that's it! You win!"

The spiritual war ended that day on October 22nd. Peace had come to reside in my heart as I put the lives of my wife and little girl into God's hands and believed that He would indeed direct our paths. Oh, and guess where I was when the peace came? It was in a little village by a reservoir and a power plant named Safe Harbor. God was helping me realize that we would be safe in His care as we became obedient to His call. And, the *power* of the Holy Spirit would be *generated* in our lives.

Weeks of indecision for Jim followed that Sunday evening service. It was a roller coaster ride for me. One day he was ready to contact Navajo Missions, the next day he felt compelled to stay where we were. Several things seemed to come up as obstacles for pursuing a ministry so far away: our families, our home, our church and Jim's job, which he loved.

We came from two very close families, with all our siblings living within a short drive from one another. Jim's sister, Mary Elizabeth, had ventured the furthest, but still lived within an hour's drive. Jim's parents still lived in his childhood home and the majority of our two families worshipped together in the same church each week. My sister, Donna, had experienced more health problems over the years. Now married, with two children, Donna had been through several surgeries on her leg. The problems she had experienced while a teenager, had now been diagnosed as cancer. The same month Jim Snare had visited our church, Donna had faced surgery again – this time resulting in her left leg being amputated at the hip. I felt a responsibility to helping her and her family, in a way I could not if we were to move. We felt safe, secure, needed and loved in our present surroundings. How were we to leave that?

We enjoyed our nice three-bedroom home. We had fond memories of raising Lisa in this home and we weren't sure how good it would be to disrupt her from all that she knew as home. We were double-minded people who wanted God's will for our lives, but we needed divine direction in order to know what God's will was for us.

Jim was not only one of the top salesmen in his district, he was leading people to Christ. He found his job to be an avenue for sharing what God had done for mankind by sending His Son Jesus to earth. He enjoyed coming home at night and sharing ways he had witnessed to those he visited that day.

Our church, Lancaster First Church of God, was not only our place of worship each week, but the catalyst of our social life, too. We belonged to a group of peers who loved the Lord and spent many fun times together.

Some were childhood friends, others came into our group through marriage. They were an awesome support to us spiritually, as well as emotionally as we all raised our young children together.

But the night Jim crawled into bed and said, "I believe we are to sell the house," I knew there was no turning back. He had heard from the Lord and our lives were going to change forever.

That evening after praying with Kay we felt the peace of God settle into our hearts. I wrote a letter to the President of Navajo Missions, Jack Drake. I told him of our encounter with the Snares and how God was moving in our lives. I mentioned that we believed God was calling us to work with Navajo children, but we didn't know what that would look like or when that would happen. A few days later the phone rang. It was Jack Drake calling from Farmington, New Mexico to let us know they needed houseparents!

We weren't ready for a quick response like that. Before the call ended, he wanted to know when we could come to Farmington for a personal interview. I looked at Kay and said, "I guess the time has come to talk to our families about God's call in our lives." I remember talking with my parents about the possibility of moving to New Mexico. My mom thought that Haiti sounded closer than New Mexico. In actuality, she was right. Farmington was about 500 miles further away than Haiti. But, contrary to the beliefs of some, you don't need a passport to go to New Mexico. It actually became one of our 50 states in 1912.

More phone calls and letters led to our fact-finding flight to Farmington at the beginning of January, 1975. Our flight from Denver was on the reliable workhorse of the sky, the Frontier Airlines Convair 580. These jet-prop planes were quite versatile as they flew over the rugged Rocky Mountain region, which we found out, could provide quite a bit of turbulence. We had one stop in Alamosa, Colorado on our way to Farmington. The weather report the day before our trip mentioned that Alamosa had the lowest temperature in the country at -2 degrees.

It was a late Sunday afternoon when we landed in Farmington. As we taxied to the terminal, light snow was falling. We looked out the window and saw a man standing next to the fence bundled up with a long overcoat, scarf and hat to protect him from the cold winter winds. From the pictures I had seen, I was sure it was Jack Drake. As we greeted him I was careful not to say, "Hi Jack!" Remember, this was in the 1970s when people were still hi-jacking airplanes.

The airport in Farmington sits on a flat mesa overlooking the city. Both ends of the runway have shear drop-offs. Many of the pilots jokingly call the airport the "S.S. Farmington" because it looked like an aircraft carrier. Navajo Missions could actually be seen from the airport as we made our way down the hill. Like many visitors who come to the mission, we thought the ministry would be located out of town on the Navajo Reservation. To our surprise, in less than 10 minutes, we drove onto the campus from the four-lane highway known as West Main Street.

The horseshoe shaped dirt driveway took us by several buildings, four of which were designated for care of the children. We stopped in front of a mobile home, which was Jack and Betty Drake's residence. We hurriedly had some light supper with them before they took us off to Emmanuel Baptist Church in town. While the mission was interdenominational, this was the church where all the houseparents attended with their children. Jack was actually one of the pastors who preached in the church in the early days when they met in an apple shed several miles outside of Farmington.

After the service Jack and Betty dropped us off at a little motel about a half mile down the street from the mission. All the beds were filled with kids at the mission, so we stayed at the motel at night for our weeklong visit. Each morning we would walk to the mission and have breakfast with the Drakes.

I never ate much for breakfast, but Betty cooked a hearty meal each morning and I readily ate it. One morning, we arrived at their home to find a big pot of oatmeal waiting for us. This would be a challenge for me, as I disliked hot cereals of any kind, especially oatmeal. Wanting to be gracious, I accepted a bowl filled with oatmeal and brown sugar. I was so grateful when I finally saw the bottom of the bowl and felt rather victorious about being able to finish my serving. Jim remarked on how good the oatmeal was and I politely agreed. With that, Betty quickly added another scoop of oatmeal to my bowl, assuring us there was still plenty to be eaten. Those were the last two bowls of oatmeal I would ever eat!

The rest of our meals were eaten in the various homes, which gave us opportunities to see these large families in action. It was amazing to see each child fulfilling their individual responsibilities of setting the table, pouring milk into glasses, helping little ones into chairs and getting themselves seated to begin the meal. After the meal, the children continued their chores of clearing the table, sweeping the floor, loading the dishwasher and sitting down to homework. I was mesmerized as I watched these busy families function like a well-oiled machine.

After the evening meal, we would talk with the house-parents and their older children. We were interested in the teenagers' view of the Mission, what they liked or disliked about living there, and what they wanted to do in the future. Since many of the teens were girls, it was easy to get them to talk and share their feelings. One message was clear from most of them. They didn't like it when they had to change houseparents. They wanted people for houseparents who had a long-term commitment.

The first house built at the mission in 1953 was a two-story home and it was filled with 17 kids! Throughout the evening we would take in the organized chaos in this over-loaded home. The bedrooms were filled with bunks and additional mattresses were placed in a corner of the living room and in the hallways. Apparently they had received new children in recent weeks and since construction of the fourth house was not yet finished, they tried to make room for them. This was one of the reasons why Jack's phone call was rather straightforward when he said, "We need houseparents!" In the days ahead, we would con-template our ability to be competent houseparents "with a long-term committent."

Early in the week a snow storm blew through the area. There was just an inch or two of snow in Farmington, so Jack wanted to show us what the mountains to the north in Colorado looked like after a snowfall. Off we went in his big old two-tone blue Oldsmobile Delta 88. As we neared Durango, Colorado it was evident the snowfall there was quite substantial, nearly covering the top of the fence posts.

We would have been content with that one-hour trip, but Jack wanted us to see the mountains up close and personal. What a magnificent sight to view these rugged San Juan Mountains with peaks topping 14,000 feet. We definitely weren't in Pennsylvania any more! Onward we traveled north for another 25 miles until we saw the sign for the Purgatory Ski Resort. It was in that parking lot where the wheels of that heavy Oldsmobile began to spin wildly in the deep snow. Kay and I got out and slipped and slided to the back of the car and began pushing, but to no avail. Before long, a couple of young men dressed in colorful ski attire joined us and the car was free.

The following day Jack took us 125 miles through the Navajo reservation to Gallup, New Mexico. Just 30 miles west of Farmington, in Shiprock, the two-lane road crossed over the San Juan River (one of three rivers flowing through Farmington). The town of Shiprock (Navajo: Tsé Bit'aí, "rock with wings" or "winged rock") is named for the volcanic core rock formation rising above the desert floor.

The hundred miles of highway from Shiprock to Gallup included dips in the road on a regular basis. Jack said they were there to carry the water across the road during flash floods, which happened mainly in the summer when thunderstorms rolled across the desert. We also noticed many Navajos hitch-hiking along the road. While alcohol was not permitted on the reservation, we saw many bottles and cans strewn along the road. On occasion we noticed sheepherders watching over their flocks, along with the assistance of their loyal sheep dogs.

I just couldn't fathom what the sheep were eating from this desolate, dry desert.

While the trip to Gallup was an eye-opening experience for us as we took in the lifestyle and landscape of the Navajo people, Jack was actually going to Gallup to attend the funeral of a Navajo man killed in a drunk-driving car accident. Before the service we went with Jack to the hospital in Gallup where he was visiting one of the survivors. As we sat down in the crowded waiting room, we looked at the faces of the Diné (the Navajo People). There were lots of kids, parents and grandparents. Kay and I quickly realized we were in the minority, the only Anglo people in the room. We could not help but notice the patience of those waiting for their appointments. No one seemed to be in a hurry as they visited with one another in their Navajo language.

From there we went to the funeral held in a small church out on a sandstone mesa. We were there on time, but we were about the only ones in the church. We soon got our first lesson about how the Native American people consider time. It can be described as cyclical, present oriented, and "in the moment." Their attitude toward time is relaxed and unhurried. They tend to live their day within a general window of time around natural events like sunset or meals. This was certainly "foreign" to our upbringing in Pennsylvania, where we showed up early for events and services. To our surprise, about 30 minutes later the church was filled to overflowing.

Before we left Pennsylvania on this trip, we had prayed God would reveal His will to us, letting us know if this was the place where He wanted us to serve. On Wednesday of our interview week, Jack took us to meet Dick Ullrich, the Chairman of the Board. He was a petroleum engineer whose office was on the fourth floor of the El Paso Natural Gas district office. After meeting with him, I realized that it was not only Jack Drake who had committed his life to this ministry. Dick was not just a board chairman in name only. He regularly met with Jack and every Saturday morning would come out to the mission to pray with him.

We really liked the emphasis that was placed on prayer. Every weekday morning the staff would gather in the office for 30 minutes of devotion and prayer time. Each Thursday evening there was Bible study for the children and also prayer and Bible study for the adults. These were some of the attributes that we were looking for in a ministry and we came to the decision we would come to Navajo Missions if they decided to accept us.

Before we left New Mexico, we shared our desire to join the staff if Jack and the Board agreed to have us come. As we made our way across the country we realized that we had just made a huge commitment. We had earlier turned down the possibility of being dorm parents at a Navajo mission school in the region because it was evident that they were only looking for a nine-month commitment. If we were going to move across the country, we desired a long-term position where we could actually invest our lives and, hopefully, see the results of our efforts, with God's leading.

Kay's parents picked us up in Baltimore and we anxiously drove the two hours back to Lancaster County. This was the longest time we had been away from our 3-year-old daughter, Lisa. She had spent the time with my parents and, of course, enjoyed all the attention grandparents provide their grandkids. After spending a week away from her, we were ready to get our little family back together again.

We told both of our parents that we had a good, positive experience and offered to join their staff, but would wait to see what the days ahead held for us. We wouldn't have to wait days. No sooner had we carried our luggage into our home when the phone rang. It was Jack Drake calling. He said, "We've talked and prayed about your visit with us. We realize you are rather young, (I was 27 and Kay was 25) but we believe God would have you come and serve with us." His call confirmed God's call in our lives.

The next few months were filled with excited anticipation for us as we began to plan for our move to Navajo Missions. My parents were cautiously optimistic about our call to mission work, although my mom was pretty teary-eyed initially.

One of my first actions concerning our move was to meet with my Fuller Brush Sales Manager and inform him of our calling to the Navajo. I remember meeting with Gordon in his second-floor office in one of the old office buildings in downtown Lancaster. I didn't expect the meeting to last very long, but the more I shared about God's call the more interested he became in my personal relationship with Christ. He was curious about what would motivate a successful salesman to give up his profession and move across the country. As I shared my faith with him, he shared his desire to know Christ in the same way that I did. When I asked him if he would like to pray and ask Christ to become Lord of his life, he said, "I sure would!"

As I left his office that rainy Monday morning, my feet were barely hitting the steps or sidewalk. God was already confirming His call in my life. Even the bright yellow parking ticket under my windshield wiper could not dampen my spirits on this day.

We had a house to sell. We had lots of things that wouldn't fit in the U-Haul trailer. So, we began selling items that wouldn't be needed in the house where we would begin our houseparenting ministry. We had a yard sale, too. Before we left the mission, we asked Jack if there were specific items that would be needed for our work. He said they needed an 8-12 passenger van for our house and he was sure that Kay would like to have a dishwasher for her large family of children. Kay's dad had a mechanic friend who owned a low-mileage Ford Econo-line van that we got for a good price. A call from Kay's aunt revealed they were updating their kitchen and wondered if we could use their old dishwasher. One item at a time, we saw God checking off the items needed before our move in April. His faithfulness was overwhelming to us.

One of the big questions we had concern about was our ability to raise the necessary monthly funds needed for our income of $725 per month. While that wasn't an abundant income, we did have free housing and food to go along with up to 10 kids. So, we spoke with our pastor, Bill Wagner, to see if we could present our needs to the church. He heartily agreed. We were given a special Sunday evening service to show some of our slides taken during our interview and share the work that we would be doing.

Our church was always a mission-minded church and welcomed the possibility of having two more of their own move out to the mission field. While the other missionaries supported by our church were in the foreign lands of India, Bangladesh and Pakistan, we would be ministering to poverty-stricken people (the Navajo) living in the desolate desert lands in the Four Corners region of our country.

While discussion and questions continued for a while after our presentation, there was one lady who stood to her feet and commanded the attention of those who had gathered. It was Pauline Malehorn. As she spoke, she reminded us   of the Navajo grandmas we met on our visit to New Mexico. Once or twice a year she would even dress like the Navajos, including a pleated full skirt with velveteen blouse and abundant jewelry.

As she stood to speak that evening, all ears were attentive to her words. She said, "My husband and I spent many years in Farmington with the Navajos. They are a beautiful people who have great needs. Jack Drake, the founder of Navajo Missions, once worked with us at the Mission School. He was a dedicated missionary who loved the Navajo so much that he began the home for children in 1953 to provide homes for the youngsters who needed a safe place to live. That mission is less than a mile from where we served. The Bakers have found a good place to serve. And I think our church should support them."

And, with that said, Kay and I were dismissed from the meeting. The church body was ready to vote on our support. It was overwhelmingly agreed that they would provide $725 per month for our support! Kay and I were humbled and elated that our church family would be willing to consider us worthy of their support. We knew their prayers would follow us just as faithfully as their financial gifts. Today, our home church, Lancaster First Church of God, continues to support us financially, never missing a month of support over the past 40 years. When people inquire about the length of our ministry at The Mission, we are always eager to tell them of the faithfulness of our church family in Pennsylvania. Their prayers, friendship, visits and encouragement over the years played a vital role in our ability to work through the hard times and stay faithful to God's call.

In the early winter of 1975 a special Sunday evening Commissioning service was held for us at our church. In addition to our local congregation, officials from our denomination offices in Findlay, Ohio participated in the service. Because our denomination was exploring possibilities of starting a mission work in Navajoland, they were excited to have us on the ground in New Mexico to explore additional opportunities for work among the Native Americans. Little did we know then that we would actually make those connections that would later become a fruitful Church of God ministry in three different locations in the Navajo Nation.

At the end of the service, Kay and I and Lisa were asked to come to the altar for a special time of prayer. There were several who prayed, but I can only remember the words of our pastor's wife, Jean, when she prayed, "Lord, we're not just giving our used clothing to missions. Tonight we are giving our best … this young family who has heard Your call and is obediently responding by leaving us to serve You through their care of Navajo boys and girls."

It was at this same altar that Kay and I both knelt as youngsters to ask Jesus to forgive us of our sins and help us to live for Him. It was at this same altar where we would join our hands and hearts together in marriage. This altar was the place where we joined many others during that special Lay-Witness Mission weekend and fully committed our lives to His service. And, it was at this altar we dedicated our baby daughter, Lisa, to God asking Him to use us to be the examples of Godly love and direction to her, and help her to also live for Him.

Those decisions we made at that altar would cause us to *alter* our lives and serve Him during the next 40 years among our new neighbors, the Navajo.

Chapter Seven

LESSONS IN PATIENCE

As we entered the western side of Farmington on April 10, 1975 we slowed our van and trailer to make the wide turn into the Mission grounds. The large wooden sign included the words, "Visitors Welcome," which is what we were when we came onto the grounds the first time. Now we were becoming the residents who would welcome others onto these grounds in the years to come.

The house we were told we would be moving into for our houseparenting duties had changed since our initial visit. So, we pulled our van up to the first house on the grounds to begin our task of unloading all of our earthly possessions. Before long Jack and Betty Drake were there to greet us along with several of the staff members and children. It was then that Jack informed us that the couple who were currently houseparents in the home we were to move into had gotten delayed in their moving plans to the church out-station near Gallup, New Mexico. So, plan B (maybe standing for Baker) was put into effect.

Other staff members met us and helped unload our U-Haul trailer into the large living room of the house that we would eventually call our home. Then we were shown a small one-bedroom trailer down the sidewalk that we could live in until our designated home was available. While this wasn't what we signed up for, we knew that God was again stretching our faith and perseverance as we began our new life as missionaries.

As we awaited our move into the large home where we could begin our ministry as houseparents, I became quite involved with a combination of maintenance duties, which included spackling and painting in a fourth children's home on the campus. I also became involved in activities in the Mission Print shop. My experiences in printing in Pennsylvania were helpful as I learned how to operate the offset presses. Another ministry of the mission was called Dial-A-Blessing. A two-minute phone devotional meditation was put on for a week at a time. I was asked to put a message on for the week and chose to share the 4 Spiritual Laws. By the end of the week several called indicating their need for Jesus.

As the days of waiting to get into our new home stretched into weeks, we became quite frustrated. Our patience was being stretched. We were anxious to begin our care of children. Finally, six weeks after our arrival we were able to help this family move from the mission in Farmington to the out-station in Gallup, where they would help an older missionary couple with pastoral work. What a relief to finally move into this large, six-bedroom house and welcome our first of many Navajo boys and girls into our home.

The trailer we were in consisted of a small living room, kitchen, bath and bedroom. We would put Lisa to sleep in our bedroom at night, then move her to the living room when we were ready to go to bed. Our miniature long-haired dachshund, Gretel, would find one of our beds to sleep in, too. One night I was sitting with my back to the window. My dad had called on the phone and I was excitedly telling him we would soon be moving into the house where we would be houseparents. Suddenly, a strange noise caused me to turn my head and look out of the window. There stood a cow on our porch! Laughing hysterically, I told my dad what was happening. "I bet you never thought I would have a cow standing on my front porch," I said to Dad. He laughed and said "No, but I never thought I would have Navajo grandchildren either." We would soon find out chasing cows, at all hours of the day or night, would become part of Jim's job description, too.

Lisa was already beginning to make friends with some of the children in the other homes. The first night we arrived, a Thursday, the children were gathering in another home for Bible Study. Two of the children scheduled to move into our home when we became houseparents, Valerie and Geri, each took Lisa's hand and off to Bible Study she went with them. She never looked back. She had just begun her journey as a missionary's kid.

During our interview in January, I had toured the home we thought we would be moving into upon our arrival. In my mind, I had arranged our furniture and set up bedrooms. With the latest decision to move us into a different home, I was aware I had never been any further than the living room. The rest of the home was a mystery to me until we were able to move in six weeks later. After a brief tour, I immediately knew God had planned this home for us.

When we lived in Pennsylvania, I occasionally mentioned to Jim three things I would enjoy having in a house, if we were ever to build another home. My tour of our "new home" in Farmington revealed all three things. Imagine my shock and surprise when I discovered a laundry room beside the kitchen, a playroom next to the family room and a fireplace in the kitchen. For the next 18 years, I would enjoy these three "gifts" that I knew only God could put together. I saw them as a daily blessing from a loving God who knew the desires of my heart. He had prepared a "special order" home just for me.

We were not only ecstatic about moving into the home God had provided, but to also begin caring for the children who had brought us to Navajo Missions. Already living in the home were two brothers, Joey and Robbie (ages 6 and 5). With their former houseparents now moving to Gallup, they were a little confused about us moving into "their" home. They soon got involved in helping to unpack our boxes and greet the other children who were moving into the home.

Valerie and Geri, ages 7 and 6, had grown up at the mission since they were babies. Although not biological sisters, they had lived in the same home for most of their lives, being raised by a single lady, Colleen Turner. It was a new experience for them to have a husband and wife as houseparents. During the first few weeks, we would sometimes hear a knock on our bedroom door early in the morning. It would be Valerie. She would open the door and we would ask her what she needed. She would reply, "nothing, I'm just looking." This would happen several times before we realized she was becoming comfortable with seeing both of us in the same bed.

Geri was very dependent upon Valerie as her "big sister." Colleen had also worked in the office during the day, so it was different for Geri to now have a housemom who was home all day. She slowly began transferring her dependence upon me as her mom. One night, as I was tucking her into bed, Geri looked at me and asked, "Who's going to be my mommy when you leave?" Her question pierced my heart and secretly I prayed to God for His strength to be the mother Geri needed, for as long as she needed. In my heart, I hoped it would be a long time. Valerie and Geri had already become protective of Lisa and asked to share a room with her. Thus began a friendship that would last into adulthood.

One of the other mission homes was overflowing with teenage girls and the decision had been made to move two of the girls into our home when we arrived. Genevieve and Caroline, two sisters ages 14 and 12, moved in on our first day, too. By evening, we gathered around the dinner table with seven children. We were experiencing the joy that most new parents experience. A "birthing" had taken place and a family was born. Over the next 16 years we would see many changes in our family. Children would come and go, but our vision of "family" would remain the same. It was our hope that each child who spent time in our home would feel like they were not only a part of our family, but also a part of the family of God.

Being the first house off the main five-lane highway in front of the mission we began to realize that there would be more than little children visiting in our home. Our first Sunday found us finishing lunch after church at our kitchen table with the children. There was a knock at the door. There stood a Navajo man with crutches. His clothing was dirty. His hair was disheveled. He definitely carried the odor of alcohol and the streets with him. He was polite as he asked, "Sir, I'm from out of town and hungry. Could you give me a sandwich and a drink of water?"

As I looked at him more closely, I realized that he was an amputee. Immediately my thoughts were drawn to Kay's sister in Pennsylvania, also an amputee. I invited him to come in and sit at our table as Kay prepared him something to eat. As we listened to his story of alcoholism we were prompted to inquire of his spiritual health. He readily admitted that he needed Jesus to take control of his life. He prayed with us and accepted Christ into his life right there at our table! As he walked away from our home toward the street, I wondered if we would be seeing him on a regular basis. We never saw him again. He was just the first of many who would pray with us over the coming years.

Two of our other visitors in those first two months were Clayton and Margery Peck. Since we had stayed in the Pecks' home during our move to New Mexico, it was nice for them to now see us settled into our new home and doing what we had been called to do. Clayton was the Chairman of the Commission on National Missions for our denomination. He was on a fact-finding trip to the Navajo Nation to see if there was a mission opportunity that could be investigated for possible mission opportunities. As it turned out, that out-station in Mentmore, near Gallup, would become the beginning of Native American Ministry for the Churches of God General Conference.

Chapter Eight

THE FIRST YEAR IS
THE HARDEST

O ur first year at Navajo Missions was an eye-
opener in many ways as we were forced to learn
so many new things in our rookie year as missionaries. It was also an eye-closer when we would lay
our heads down at the end of an 18-hour day. We were
exhausted, but also thrilled to know God had called us to
serve in this unique mission field right here in our own
country. Before we moved to Farmington, we would
often jokingly say to our friends that since our 3-year-old
daughter Lisa took up most of our time, nine more children couldn't be much harder. Like I said, "We were
rookies ... what did we know?"

Our days began at 6 a.m. moving from room to room,
getting the school-aged children up and moving toward
their bus stop destination at the front of the property.
The table was always set the night before, eliminating
some time needed to prepare for breakfast. As I prepared
food, Jim would supervise the children with their morning

chores. Each child made their own bed. One child in each room would vacuum the bedroom floor and another would take their trash to the large kitchen trash can, to be emptied in the dumpster by another child. The smaller children would go room to room and collect all the laundry, which would be delivered to the laundry room. During the day, I would wash and fold the laundry and have individual piles waiting for the children when they returned from school. (It was an unwritten rule that all laundry had to be put away in their drawers and closets before they had an after-school snack).

Then we would all sit down and enjoy breakfast together. Junior high and high school students would usually finish eating, brush their teeth and rush out the side door for the bus. The elementary students would brush their teeth and meet at the front door, where Jim or I would pray with them before they left for the bus. With the remaining 20 minutes before Jim left for the office, he would dress any babies or toddlers in the family. I would assist any pre-schoolers and begin cleaning up breakfast.

At 8 a.m. I joined other staff members at our prayer and devotion time in the building just 10 feet away from our side door. This central office building served a variety of purposes. It was home to our central kitchen, including pantry and walk-in refrigerator and freezer, print shop, dark room, offices and Christian Bookstore. It was a busy place and most days I loved it!

Some days I would be requested to help with maintenance projects that were abundant. While I wasn't by any means a "handy-man" I was handy to those who needed help with the physical jobs of the day. Sometimes, those tasks included work with animals on the small farm that took up a portion of the 12 acres of land. While I was born into a farming family, I was definitely a "green-horn" when it came to the care and feeding of animals. I still remember my feeble attempts to hold down a wiry steer for the branding procedure. And the days that we spent in the hay fields of a local ranch, gathering hay bales for the hungry herd of 50 head of cattle, were absolutely exhausting to me. Our founder Jack Drake believed the more cattle we had the less cost we would have in our food budget. I wasn't quite sure that the numbers would actually confirm that theory, but hey, I was the rookie.

Those first six months of my mission experiences also had me spending up to four days at a time at that church mission station in Mentmore. Here again I was out of my comfort zone, helping to physically build a church near Gallup. The mason was a Navajo man who was depending on me to keep the mortar mixed and coming his way. He caught my attention one day by slinging some mortar at my head as he shouted, "hashtl'ish," the Navajo word for "mud." But, at least I was beginning to learn some Navajo words. The single-wide mobile home that we slept in near the church was hot at the end of the 100-degree day. Unfortunately, my sleep was interrupted at times with the sounds of the mice running through their home.

Being separated from Kay and Lisa during those weeks was difficult. I missed being with them and hated the fact that Kay had to care for the needs of our large family by herself while I was gone. Jack often joined me on those adventures to Mentmore. He was quite the encourager and would often share the fact that "the first year of mission life is the hardest." We were discovering that to be true, but we knew that God had called us and that He would meet our every need. We found comfort in the words from the psalmist who said, "Wait on the Lord:

be of good courage, and he shall strengthen your heart." (Psalms 27:14 NKJV)

As our first summer came to a close, the roof was on the church building and services had begun with the new pastor, Richard Langner. He was the former housedad in the home we moved into at the mission. With less than 5 percent of Navajos professing Christ as savior, these small churches scattered across the Navajo Nation were instrumental in bringing the hope of Jesus to those who had not yet realized Christ's love. It was a blessing to be a part of that dedication service later in the year and see many Navajo families stream in the doors to hear the "Good News."

Back in Farmington, my days were occupied more and more in the print shop. In addition to printing promotional brochures and letters for the mission, we were printing lots of booklets that taught the Navajos how to read their language. Wycliffe Bible Translators assisted a local group of missionaries, including David and Goldie Tutt, with the first printing of the New Testament in Navajo. This local committee worked diligently, eventually translating the Old Testament as well. Our print shop and bookstore became a distribution center for many of these materials including several thousand hymnals. Volunteers would gather regularly to help assemble these items by hand.

Many of those who were on staff had come from other areas of the country to serve as missionaries. But there were also Navajo people on staff who were helping to reach their own people with the Gospel. Paul Johnson was one of them. When we arrived, Paul had been living in a tiny trailer on the grounds for the previous 10 years. Mowing lawns, assembling Navajo song books and reading materials, putting up the American flag each morning, and taking it down each evening, Paul came to serve.

Paul loved to share his faith in Christ with anyone who would listen, whether it was an alcoholic living on the streets or in a church service across the Navajo Reservation. He too was an alcoholic at one time. He said, "Before I met Christ I had no hope at all." After his parents died, he was raised by his grandparents ... without Christ. He said, "I grew up with fear and superstitions. Anytime I heard someone crying at night, I thought evil spirits were coming to get me." I admired Paul, who was most comfortable speaking his Native tongue. At times he would listen to me speaking with my Pennsylvania Dutch accent and just smile as he went about his work.

We were quite a diverse group of missionaries from various areas of the country. Several were from the Michigan area, Jack Drake's homeland. Another couple was from Alabama. I was fascinated with their accent and phrases that included comments like, "I got the kids to crawl into the van and carried them across town."

I continued to learn much about mission life from Jack Drake. He was one of the most humble men I have ever met. When visitors would compliment him on the work he was accomplishing he would often say, "Well, I have found if I can get people to work for us who are smarter than I am, then I'm not so bad off myself." He would welcome the advice of those who labored with him, realizing that everyone had talents and abilities that God could use. I was always shocked and honored when he would ask my opinion on the workings of the mission and how I thought things could be improved.

Jack had a great sense of humor and enjoyed telling some of his stories over and over again to folks who came by. More than once he would get so tickled with a story that he would turn red with laughter. One of his favorite words was, "Wow," which he stretched into a nine-letter word – "Wooooooow," after hearing a praise report or, just as easily, after hearing of a tragedy. He was always ready to pray for anyone, anytime. He had a heart of compassion and would get up in the middle of the night to take a stranded traveler to his home on the reservation land.

When we were considering coming to the mission I asked him if it would be good for me to attend Bible College prior to our arrival. He assured me that God would take me just as I was and that he would provide personalized Bible and ministry training that he had learned during his seven years at Moody Bible Institute and Wheaton College. He reminded me that God often doesn't call the qualified, but He qualifies the called! So, I was pleased to have him as my mentor. Jack was quick to believe that I had business and administrative abilities that could be an asset to the ministry in the future.

Dick Ullrich was the Chairman of the Board when we arrived. He and Jack faithfully met for prayer each Saturday morning in the Mission office. On those Saturday mornings, Dick would hear of Jack's experiences during the past week with staff and discuss the ministry in general. He was a deeply spiritual man who also served in a leadership role with the local Full Gospel Business Men's Fellowship. Little did I know then that Jack and Dick were praying for God to bring a young man to the mission who would perhaps one day become the successor to Jack.

One of the blessings of working at Navajo Missions was the fact that Kay and I could work together as a team caring for our large family of children. While I would spend much of my day in the print shop, office or helping with maintenance projects, I was always ready to help out with the many duties that accompanied the title, "housedad."

Our house was the only home of the four children's homes that was all on one floor. The other three homes were two-story, which limited the houseparents in the amount of smaller children they could have in their homes. We quickly became the home for the overflow of pre-schoolers, which kept us busy from morning until night – sometimes even into the night.

About six months into our first year, Byron, 23 days old, came into our home. His mother and grandmother brought him to the mission and Jack placed him in our care. Although I was sure I was about two months pregnant, we hadn't made that known to the staff. When our news became common knowledge, there was discussion about moving Byron to another home. By that time, we had bonded with this little guy – he was part of our family.

For about five months, Byron grew physically, but seemed very small for his age. I worried about his health, but he was getting good reports from his doctor each month. By seven months, Byron only weighed 11 pounds, 7 ounces. I knew something wasn't right. I asked permission to take Byron to a pediatrician in town. The pediatrician suspected Cystic Fibrosis. After a series of tests and x-rays, it was determined Byron was having a negative reaction to the formula he was on, resulting in nearly complete dehydration. With milk and diet change, we began seeing an improvement in his health. Over the next 19 years, we would watch Byron continue to grow into a healthy, strong young man, as he lived in our home.

A month later, our son, David James Baker, was born on May 4, 1976. Weighing 8 pounds and 4 ounces, David brought new joy and excitement into our lives. He was perfect in every way and I could not wait to share him with the rest of the family, including our loved-ones in Pennsylvania. Our natural family felt complete with his arrival and his five year old sister, Lisa, quickly claimed him as "hers."

In those days, hospitals were not quick to send new mothers home. My birthday was going to be two days later and I wanted to be able to bring David home by that time. The day after he was born, I asked the doctor if I would be going home the next day. He looked at Jim and asked two questions: "Do you have other children at home and will you have any help with the baby?" Jim quickly told him we had 11 other children at home and we would have PLENTY of help. Against his best judgment, the doctor let me go home the following day. Life would continue to be very exciting as we entered our second year at Navajo Missions.

Chapter Nine

PUTTING DOWN ROOTS

April 10, 1976 marked one year since we arrived at Navajo Missions. While it was a special day for us as we realized we made it through our first year, it was a much more impactful day for the Navajos. Jack and I drove just five miles south of the mission winding our way up the road that took us to the top of the dramatic sandstone cliffs known as "the bluffs" that provide a panoramic view of the Farmington valley that includes the confluence of the Animas, San Juan and La Plata Rivers known as "Totah" (among the rivers) to the Navajos. To the north you can also see the La Plata Mountains, 60 miles away near Durango, Colorado.

Our purpose on this day was to join nearly 8,000 Navajos on the fields of the Navajo Agricultural Products Industry (NAPI). This was the day that the Navajos would celebrate the completion of the three promises of the Treaty of 1868 that was signed by Chief Barboncito. The U.S. government promised to provide schools, medical clinics and hospitals and irrigated land to the Navajos.

The Boarding School system with its less than favorable success and medical facilities were providing needed service to this land of 150,000 people. Finally, over 100 years after the signing of the treaty our government was providing the beginning of irrigated land in this parched region that averages just 8 inches of rain per year.

As the crowd gathered by the first pumping station, Navajo Chairman Peter McDonald recalled Barboncito's prophetic words after their tragic Long Walk, "After we get back to our country it will brighten up again, and the Navajos will be happy as the land. Black clouds will rise and there will be plenty of rain. Corn will grow in abundance and everything will look happy." When the huge sprinklers were turned on the people ran underneath them like children running through the sprinklers on their lawn. I can still remember seeing the Navajo grandmas dressed in their finest garments and jewelry under the sprinklers with their hands raised in thanks and praise.

I couldn't help but think of the "Living Water" that we were now sharing with our Navajo neighbors. How thankful we were that we could play a part in helping to revive a thirsty nation. "Water will gush forth in the wilderness and streams in the desert. The burning sand shall become a pool, the thirsty ground bubbling springs ... And a highway will be there; and it shall be called the Holy Way." (Isaiah 35:6-8) Each day as we awoke and served Christ here, we realized that we were becoming more rooted in this ministry of hope to some of our First Americans, the Navajo.

While Navajo Missions is not located on the Navajo Reservation land, most of the children who came into our homes came from families that lived in humble dwellings located within the boundaries of the 27,000 square mile reservation that was located in parts of three states. Farmington, known as a border town (along with Gallup, New Mexico, Flagstaff and Page, Arizona) has benefitted economically from the many Navajo families that come here to shop, especially on weekends. Alcohol is prohibited on the reservation land. Unfortunately, many liquor establishments are located adjacent to the borders which have provided easy access causing much pain and suffering over the years. Nearly all of the children in our care were from families who were dealing with addiction issues.

It was my desire to learn as much as possible about the Navajo (the Diné). Of course, Jack Drake shared many of his experiences with me during that first year, but I also enjoyed hearing from the Navajos themselves about their culture and the challenges that they faced. One of those trusted friends was Fred Yazzie. He was born in Shiprock, New Mexico, educated at Taylor University and ordained at Asbury Theological Seminary. He was converted and called to the ministry in his sophomore year at the Navajo Methodist Mission School in Farmington where Jack began his ministry to the Navajo as a Bible teacher.

Fred also served on the board of Navajo Missions. Fred said, "My wife taught school where many of the mission children attended. She could see the bond of the family relationships that our children had and was impressed with their good discipline." The mission assisted Fred in his ministry by donating Navajo Bibles and other literature that he used in teaching Navajos to read their own language.

When asked what he thought were the biggest obstacles in presenting the gospel to the Navajos he said, "There is a constant battle between the good and bad spirits. Those who are traditional in their beliefs believe in animism. They tend to worship the creation instead of the Creator. They have many fears and superstitions that keep them in bondage. There are others who use peyote, a cactus bud, in their ceremonies. They have hallucinations, saying they communicate with the deity. This group calls their worship, The Native American Church."

Fred went on to share with me the fear that many have as they get involved with witchcraft. "These ceremonial gatherings are led by the medicine man. I remember as a little boy seeing feathers that were on the ground suddenly stand on end about four inches off the ground and start dancing up and down as the medicine men were singing. As the drums beat, the feathers would be in rhythm with drums." Fear is prevalent in the lives of many. If an owl continually shows up around a home, it is a sign of death coming to one of their family.

Fred was hopeful, though, as he shared with me. He saw the younger generation becoming more educated and turning away from the fear and bondage that has gripped this largest tribe of Indians, the Navajo, for generations. I was encouraged to see Fred's courage and determination as a young Navajo pastor reaching out to his own people in his own language with the Good News.

I was more determined than ever to do what I could through Navajo Missions to assist Navajos like Fred in their ministry. We would continue to provide literature through our Print Shop and Christian Bookstore. We had also begun to distribute cassettes of God's Word in Navajo. We would continue to provide safe homes for the children who were facing hardship or danger within their natural families.

I also realized that if we were going to reach more Navajos with the Good News, we needed to reach more people across the country with the stories and challenges facing these "First Americans." At that time we were producing a monthly 8-page newspaper called Navajo Trails. It was a simple publication using black and white photos that we developed in the darkroom of our Print Shop. Staff members would take turns submitting stories. The printing was done in Cortez, Colorado. Eventually, we had the printing done at our local Daily Times newspaper office.

I really believed that we needed assistance in producing a more professionally done publication if we were going to effectively tell our stories to supporters and prospective friends across the nation. It was then that we heard of Bill Armstrong, who lived in Tulsa, Oklahoma. This talented journalist was producing articles and magazines for several Christian organizations. We contracted with him to come to the Mission a few times each year gathering stories and taking many of the photos.

About two years later, when his work load increased, Bill suggested we make use of his son, Bob Armstrong, who was also a talented writer and ordained minister. That was the beginning of a lasting relationship with Bob, who made dozens of trips to the Mission over the next 20-plus years. In addition to producing the greatly improved colorful publications, his crazy sense of humor and passion for sharing God's love all over the world, resulted in Bob becoming one of my treasured friends.

Then I began thinking about Christian radio. There was no Christian station in the Four Corners area. Was God stirring that desire I had in Pennsylvania to start a Christian radio station? Only God knew for sure, but I was willing to be used of Him to bring hope into the airwaves if that was His will. By the end of our first year, the board of directors decided that I should be given the title of Mission Manager. I was happy to be a housedad to boys and girls. I certainly hadn't anticipated a leadership position at the Mission.

As we approached the end of school in 1976, we were excitedly planning our first "vacation" trip with our kids to Pennsylvania. David would be six weeks old and I was eager to introduce him to all of our family. At this point in time, we had 12 children, including David. It was our first of several times to truly be a Bakers' dozen, and then some! But, that was a challenge because our van only seated 12 passengers.

However, God had His plan in place that not only freed up space in the van for our trip, but also brought spiritual freedom to the father of some of our kids. We had five children from one family in our home. Their father, who often shared with us that he served under General Patton in the war, along with the children's step mom, came to talk about taking their five children home with them when school was out the end of May.

The kids had prayed for their father's salvation and that night, as Jack and Jim visited with him, he accepted Christ as his savior. Two of his older children also had made professions of faith while they were with us. As May came to a close, we prepared for the five children to leave our care. We would soon find out this was the most difficult part of being houseparents. These were the first children to leave our home and the experience was very painful. While we were glad the children could return to their father and home, we were saddened for the void their departure left in our family.

A week later, we were returning to our homeland, traveling with seven children, ranging in ages from 6 weeks old to 14 years old. The trip would include lots of opportunities to reunite with family and friends, as we camped out for four weeks in our parents' homes. Having never been out of the Four Corners area, our two oldest girls experienced their first days of over 100 degree temperatures with 100 percent humidity. The children all enjoyed new experiences and new foods. They loved the attention that was poured into their lives through our family and friends. David was passed around from one person to another, everyone wanting to meet and love on him. Lisa enjoyed playing with her cousins, and hearing everyone comment on how much she had grown. It was good to be home.

The trip would also have us speaking in churches in five states, sharing the ministry of Navajo Missions, as we traveled to and from Pennsylvania. But the highlight of the trip was returning to that familiar altar at Lancaster First Church of God, on a Sunday morning, to have David and Byron dedicated to the Lord, just as we had done with Lisa when she was a baby. There, with the strength and wisdom of the Lord, we dedicated ourselves to being the faithful parents we knew God wanted us to be.

Chapter Ten

A WING AND A PRAYER

B y the end of 1976 we had two housedads on our staff who were certified pilots. With the Navajo Nation encompassing nearly 27,000 square miles (about the size of West Virginia), we began to consider the possibility of acquiring a used airplane to assist missionaries and evangelists as they ministered to the Navajo. We also envisioned the plane providing emergency flights to area hospitals. Literature and other supplies could also be delivered to remote areas, saving many hours of travel.

Our newest housedad, Al Sanchez, mentioned this need to his former employer in Denver. After a visit to the Mission, this man promised to help locate a plane for our purposes. Before long he notified us that he found a used Cessna 180 aircraft. It was a tail-dragger aircraft with bigger tires suitable for the rough terrain dirt airstrips that were scattered across the reservation lands. Eventually, we gave the plane a name–The Love Dove.

While flying into the wild blue yonder in a small airplane wasn't my idea of a good time, I did have a passion to provide ways for people to soar in their relationship with Christ. One of those opportunities was "Here's Life America," an evangelistic campaign sponsored by Campus Crusade. I agreed to co-chair with Bible Translator David Tutt, as regional coordinators.

The catch phrase of the campaign was "I Found It!" which resulted in this message being proclaimed on billboards, newspaper ads and bumper stickers. More than 150 volunteers worked together during a four-week period and basically called everyone in our local phone book, giving them the opportunity to accept Christ. The "office" for the campaign was in one of the bedrooms in our home. Day and night we would have volunteers come into our home to make their calls. During that month, 320 individuals actually accepted the Lord and were enrolled in home Bible studies! Seeing people come to Christ was one of my passions in life. And, to help others experience the joy of leading someone to Christ was an added blessing.

My daytime hours of work became more and more involved with general management of the Mission ministries, which included producing promotional materials and looking for new ways to communicate our programs to existing and potential donors. It was second nature for me to constantly be thinking about new and creative ways to increase awareness and support. One of our board members, Ken Campbell, who was then President of Sunwest Bank in Farmington, characterized the Mission as "a quiet miracle on West Main Street." I was determined to do what I could to turn up the volume of this place of miracles on the west side of town.

One of those endeavors included us bringing The Rambos to town for a concert at our new Farmington

Civic Center. Buck, Dottie and their daughter, Reba, were popular gospel singers who would not only provide an evening of praise and worship, but would also bring their endorsement of Navajo Missions and the ministry taking place. Their big tour bus pulled into our dirt driveway on the morning of April 26. After visiting in our homes and offices, they prepared for our city's first major Christian concert. The auditorium quickly filled up with 1,200 people. As the curtain opened, this talented family brought a hush over the excited audience as they began singing, "We are Standing on Holy Ground." While we were excited to sponsor this inspirational evening for our city, we were overwhelmed to see dozens of people stream to the stage to make decisions for Christ. This was just the beginning of many more concerts that we would bring to our community. The "miracle on West Main Street" was moving across our region and many were taking notice. To God be the glory!

As the year came to a close, progress was being made in our pursuit of establishing the first Christian radio station in the Four Corners. We met with experts in the area and they advised us to apply to the FCC for a low-powered, non-commercial FM license. Pages and pages of FCC application forms were filled out and sent to Washington. We were told it would cost about $25,000 to put the station on the air. It appeared that God was moving us to take this step of faith, believing God would provide not only the dollars but the wisdom and staff that could bring this station to reality.

It was quite a productive year as we added an airplane to the ministry and began the process of establishing a Christian radio station in Farmington. But, most of our time and efforts were invested in the lives of the little ones that God was continuing to bring into our home.

The children brought us many new experiences and taught us the value of laughter, which is a great component to perseverance. With 10 or more children in our home, it was sometimes difficult to catch a few moments during the day to talk with each other. Jim and I knew communication would be a necessity if we were to run the home smoothly, but we also knew it would be a challenge. We often talked into the late hours of the night, discussing the needs of the children, sharing a funny story or just planning for the next day.

The children gave us so many opportunities to laugh. Being from Pennsylvania Dutch land, it was a common phrase to say "outen the lights" when I wanted a light turned off. Our children learned quickly what I meant, and would not hesitate to follow my request. However, upon the arrival of a new child, we laughed when we found him just standing out in the front yard. When asking what he was doing, he said he was just "out in the light." Yes, communication would become very necessary and challenging.

Our first Valentine's Day at Navajo Missions provided us another "communication" lesson. Seven year old Geri returned from school with a bag full of valentines, and eyes brimming with tears. When I asked her what had happened, she reported a student in her class had brought lollipops for all the students. Then at recess time, when the students were out of the classroom, he took all the lollipops back and stuck them in his lunch bag to take home. Trying to empathize with her disappointment, I naively said what my mother would have said to me in that circumstance, "I'm sorry, honey. He was an Indian giver, wasn't he?" Geri was quick to respond saying, "No, Mommy. He was WHITE!"

Not all of our days were joy-filled. Some days we had teenagers who ran away, causing distress to the younger ones in the home, as well as to Jim and me. We worried about them when they were gone, knowing danger lurked about, as well as temptations. We had always encouraged our children who knew the Navajo language to feel free to speak it with one another. They even seemed to enjoy teaching us some words and phrases.

One night, as we were having supper, two teenage sisters exchanged a conversation in Navajo. We paid little attention, knowing we couldn't decipher what they were saying anyway. Later in the evening, after all the children had gone to bed, we discovered the two sisters missing. We woke one of the other girls and asked if she knew when they had left and where they were planning to go. She had all the details, because the girls' plans had been the topic of their conversation at the dinner table that night. Yes, communication was a challenge.

One evening, during the first visit Jim's parents made to our home in New Mexico, these same two girls decided to take off on another adventure. Knowing it was the weekend of the Shiprock Fair, we were pretty sure they would try to catch a ride to Shiprock. Jim and I got into our van and drove a couple of miles, spotting the girls climbing into the back of a pickup truck. Jim pulled beside the truck and I told the driver the girls were runaways. He immediately pulled his truck over to the side of the road, and the girls climbed out. They weren't very happy about returning home with us.

As all four of us walked into the house, the girls went to their bedroom, voicing their anger and slamming their door. Jim's mother immediately looked at us and said, "Jim, you don't need to live this way." We understood her misgivings about our sometimes disruptive home life, but we also understood these girls needed a home and family, and God had asked us to provide it. Although the girls only stayed with us for two years, our relationship with them continued over the years and today we enjoy the friendship of these two beautiful Christian ladies.

Some days it seemed like we were one big, happy family. Other days it seemed like we were holding on "with a wing and a prayer." In moments of desperation, when we felt like we didn't know what to do next, we were comforted by the knowledge that our family, our home church family, and friends of the Mission were praying for us often. We would see many victories in the years ahead that could only be attributed to prayer and a gracious, loving Father.

Chapter Eleven

THE EXCITING SILVER
ANNIVERSARY YEAR

As the ministry grew, we continued to seek new friends who would pray for the ministry and provide funds to meet the daily needs. Before I arrived, Bob Fraley, founder of Development Associates for Christian Institutions in Tulsa, had helped Jack establish a child sponsorship program. This sponsorship program continues even to this day, providing an opportunity for friends to sponsor an individual child or one of our families. We were also looking for new ways to get our message to folks across the nation. We ran a small ad in some Christian magazines, but we needed something more visual.

In the early days a filmstrip was produced that could be used by church groups across the nation. That media progressed to slides narrated by whoever was sharing the story of the mission. Then, we heard of Spencer Cunningham in Ohio who was producing dual projector slide shows accompanied by a soundtrack of narration and music. He convinced us that to have the greatest impact on our audiences we needed a screen bigger than the average pop-up screen used in your home. So, we put together a 6-by-10 foot vinyl screen, and a frame of metal conduit pipes. The screen was strung together and stretched with bungee cords around the pipe frame. Along with the projectors and audio equipment, this was quite an ordeal to transport and assemble, but it was quite impressive.

I must admit that I really enjoyed putting the Mission programs into formats and productions that would more easily describe and promote the various ministries of the Mission. I guess my sales background was coming in handy. The year of 1978 was promising to be one of growth and excitement. This was the 25th Anniversary year of the mission! While we had some great ideas, we would be overwhelmed at times with all the work that needed to take place to make this year special as we celebrated God's blessings.

As the year began we welcomed new houseparents, Mark and Karen Frederick, to our staff. They came to us from El Paso, Texas where Mark had worked in Christian television. He also had experience in radio. It was always amazing to see how God would bring us just the right people with the needed talents at just the right time. Oh, yes, and he was a pilot, too. While Jack and I had the vision for Christian radio in the Four Corners, we lacked the knowledge of knowing the process and "language" of the broadcast industry.

And, as was often the case in those days, our houseparents pulled double duty as they cared for children and worked during the day with other projects. When Mark wasn't pursuing radio applications with the FCC, he was fixing vehicles and helping with other construction endeavors that eventually would include building two radio rooms in the corner of the maintenance garage.

Over the next 10 years, Mark and Karen would not only be co-workers as houseparents with us, they would become life-long friends. We enjoyed a camaraderie we hadn't experienced since our arrival as houseparents and their friendship and support became the glue that created a great working-relationships together. While Jim and Mark worked together in the office and radio station, Karen and I became great support for each other as busy moms.

Hectic schedules of laundry, meal planning, doctor visits, weekly shopping for the Mission kitchen and families, homework and childcare would be interrupted for a quick cup of coffee and exchanges of encouragement. When one of us would become discouraged or frustrated, the other was there to lend a shoulder to cry on. The evenings would find the four of us visiting together while the children played outdoors. Sometimes a late cup of coffee was needed to end the day and share a challenge or victory with one another.

Occasionally, Karen and I would pack up our pre-schoolers and shop together or go to the park or library. With seven or eight pre-schoolers between us, we would laugh at the funny looks or comments we received from other shoppers. Once, when we had eight children with us, including six-month-old David and 13-month-old Byron, a customer looked at my shopping cart of children and said, "Boy, you've been busy!" Little did she know!

I found a friendship with Karen that helped to ease my times of aloneness when I missed my sister, Donna, and other friends in Pennsylvania. When we lived there,

THE BAKERS' DOZEN and Then Some

I would take Lisa and visit for the day at Donna's house, or with my sister-in-law, Polly Baker. Those visits were refreshing, spiritually, emotionally and physically. We played with the kids, shopped, attended Bible Study together, made applesauce, froze corn and learned from each other the dos and don'ts of raising children. Now I had a friend in New Mexico that I could do these same things with, and I loved it.

As two young couples with very demanding schedules, we found in Mark and Karen the type of friendship described in (Ecclesiastes 4:9-12 NLT). "Two people can accomplish more than twice as much as one; they get a better return for their labor. If one person falls, the other can reach out and help. But people who are alone when they fall are in real trouble. A person standing alone can be attacked and defeated, but two can stand back-to-back and conquer. Three are even better, for a triple-braided cord is not easily broken."

Such teamwork was not always the case during our first couple of years at the mission. There were some on the staff who did not agree with Jack's leadership of the Mission and wanted Kay and I to work with them in getting him removed. They soon found out that I was not only *at* a Mission but *on* a mission to support Jack and help this place become an efficient, productive outreach to our Navajo neighbors.

Jack was very trusting of everybody. Unfortunately, there were times when Jack was blind-sided by some who would desire to join his staff. Back in those early days there was not the extensive back-ground checks that take place today. While references were called, there was usually an urgency to welcome new missionaries to the team. As Board of Directors President and Mission Manager,

Dick Ullrich and I became a personnel committee of three, along with Jack. It was actually through the urging of Dick and me that we terminated one of the couples that were causing unrest within the staff. This was the first time to take that kind of drastic action, but, sadly, it wouldn't be the last.

In the spring we hosted a Navajo Church Growth Seminar in Farmington. Our speakers included David Scates and Tom Dolaghan who were in the process of finishing their doctoral thesis at the School of Missions at Fuller Theological Seminary in California. These two had combed the expansive Navajo Reservation over two years meeting with Navajo pastors and missionaries. They had put their studies into a book, "The Navajos are Coming to Jesus."

Over 100 missionaries and pastors packed into the Chef Bernie's banquet room on the west side of town. The findings shared by these men showed that only 8 percent of the Navajos (13,300 people) attended church every Sunday. But this still left 92 percent who were not ready to commit their lives to Christ. This study showed there was spiritual growth. In 1950 a Navajo Christian would be surrounded by 44 non-Christian neighbors. But by 1978 there was one Christian for every 12.5 non-Christians! One of the major factors in this growth was the influx of new churches. In 1950 there were 35 churches across the reservation. By 1978 there were 343 churches! While many of them were pastored by Anglo missionaries, we would see those numbers reversed by 2015 with nearly all of the churches pastored by Navajos.

We were conducting two fund raising campaigns at the same time. The radio funds raised was $10,000 of the $25,000 needed. Then in the spring we kicked off a

Phone-A-Thon project to call people in our community regarding the construction of the new Communications Center. Our staff and ministry was growing and we needed more space in order to work efficiently as a team. The new Communications Center would provide a home for the radio station, administration offices, Christian Bookstore, mini-auditorium, prayer rooms and eventually a gymnasium. Nearly 200 volunteers came together to hear the vision God had given me and confirmed by both Jack and Dick Ullrich. Benjamin Hogue, Navajo Tribal Councilman and Chairman of the Mission board challenged those gathered with heartfelt words. "When making a presentation ... if you want to get action, you'll never do it by driving yourself ... you must be driven. Driven by what you ask? By the LOVE OF GOD!!"

Amazingly, the first $6,000 of the $500,000 needed for the Center was committed by Mission staff. Ground breaking was held that summer with a large crowd gathered for the event. Before long the large playground area at the front of the campus began to be dismantled to make way for the large excavating equipment that prepared the land for the construction. This was truly an exciting and exhausting time at the Mission, but there was even more to come.

While many of the Mission supporters were from all over the country, we were always delighted when they would come by the Mission for a visit when on vacation trips. They were always blessed by spending time with the children and staff members as they got to see first-hand how their donations were being used. Many of our family members had made their way across the nation and several young people from Pennsylvania also came to spend some extended time with us.

Following his graduation from college, my brother, Parke, came to spend a year at the Mission. He lived in the small trailer where Jim, Lisa and I had spent our first six weeks. With his experience of working with my dad in his shop, Parke was invaluable in the Mission printshop. He was a perfect fit as he printed needed pamphlets, letters and other materials. He also worked with local pastors in printing bulletins, obituaries, funeral and wedding programs. We loved having him be a part of our family at mealtimes and share in lots of our family activities.

My niece, Con Maser, also came to work at the Mission following her high school graduation. She lived in our home and assisted staff wherever she was needed. Office work, helping in the homes with the children, or running errands, Con was always glad to help others. She was an extra pair of hands for me in the evenings, too. She would help bathe the little ones and dress them for bed, or help with homework. It was a growing and maturing time for her and we enjoyed having her be a daily part of our lives again.

Their visits would refresh and encourage us, bringing us happy moments of shared memories and the opportunities to make new ones. No matter the length of these visits, it would always be hard to say goodbye when the time came for family and friends to return to Pennsylvania.

As we thought about our visitors who would stop on their way to Monument Valley, Grand Canyon and other landmarks in the west, we came up with the idea to conduct a week-long tour of Navajoland that would include the Four Corners National Monument (where you could stand on four states at once), Canyon De Chelly, Window Rock, (headquarters to the Navajo Nation government), Painted Desert, Grand Canyon, Monument Valley and

Aztec Indian Ruins. These supporters would also get to spend time at the Mission and even eat a meal with the children.

So, in October 1978 we hosted our first Navajoland Tour. It was sort of a celebration tour honoring the 25 years of ministry of founder, Jack Drake. Over 20 guests arrived from several states. They had a grand time as Jack, Mark Frederick and Colleen Turner of our staff helped with the driving of the vans and keeping the group on schedule. I stayed behind, preparing for the big 25th Anniversary banquet at our local Civic Center.

Our guest speaker was Zig Ziglar, billed as America's Most Versatile Speaker. More than 500 people attended. Our tour guests had seats right in front of the podium. Zig's ready wit was refreshing and his clear-cut Christian testimony was inspiring. He concluded his positive message by saying, "What I have seen at Navajo Missions today is love … Christ's love. It makes me so humble and grateful that you invited me to share with you." At the end of the evening we gave Zig his check for speaking to us that night. I was deeply touched and shocked when he immediately turned it over and endorsed it back to the Mission! I didn't know it then, but 34 years later I would be interviewing his daughter Julie on my radio show about her book, "Growing Up Ziglar."

Words of congratulations were expressed through letters from those who couldn't attend including New Mexico Governor Jerry Apodaca, Evangelists Oral Roberts and Pat Robertson, Senator Pete Domenici and others. Chairman of the Navajo Tribal Council, Peter McDonald, said, "You have provided not only spiritual leadership for our people, but also needed social services as well. Through your work many of our people have been given new opportunity for a more meaningful life." It was heartwarming to have these notable people recognize the importance of the Mission and the impact we were having with our Navajo neighbors.

As that night in October came to a close we were able to reveal the total funds generated from the recent Phone-A-Thon and commitments from those in attendance that night. We now had commitments of $37,000 toward the construction of the new Communication Center! It was an exciting year of major accomplishments, all to God's glory. While children continued to be the "heartbeat" of the Mission and our purpose for coming here, I was beginning to realize that God's call in our lives was not going to be limited to serving as houseparents. Fortunately, we were young and had lots of energy which was necessary as we put in many 18-hour days.

Kay at 3 and Jim at 5 years of age.

Right: Kay and her siblings, Donna and Parke.

Left: Kay's Parents Parke and Ruth Duing.

Jim and his parents Roy and Esther Baker with siblings,
Gene, Mary, Dan and Bob (L to R).

High School sweethearts.

Two became one
April 19, 1969.

Our early days as houseparents with Lisa and Dave.

It takes a long sub to feed a "Bakers' dozen."

All 13 dressed up for a formal photo.

Left: Early days of KNMI located in a corner of the shop.

Below: Christmas Care-A-Vans to needy families in the Navajo Nation.

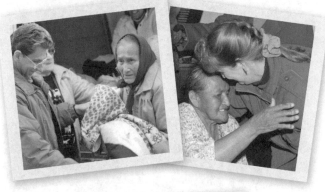

Jack Drake passes the position of President to Jim Baker in 1987.

Jim interviews Franklin Graham in 1996 during a four-day festival in Farmington.

Jim presents sacred pottery to Navajo Nation President Kelsey Begaye at Return to the Promise gathering on April 1, 2000.

Jim and Kay with Art Linkletter, who spoke at 50th Anniversary Celebration in 2003.

Jami, Breann and Lisa Chavez in 2005.

Mother's Day 2006 (Back: Dave, Kay and Byron; Front: Lisa, Geri and Valerie)

Dave and Heather Baker with Samantha (L) and Seattle (R) in 2013.

Bob Fitz, Navajo Ministries Projects Manager, began the Bi-Fly Fishing Tournament in 1994, providing thousands of dollars to the Four Corners Home for Children over the years.

Joe and Gerri Begay, Eric and Terri Fisher pose with Jim and Kay in Lancaster, Pennsylvania while in the area for fund-raising banquets and church services in 2014.

Chapter Twelve

"GOD IS BUILDING OUR BUILDING"

I n addition to providing homes to boys and girls, the mission continued to focus on meeting practical needs of destitute families living in remote areas of the Navajo Nation. Bob and Mildred Sharples joined our ministry team in 1978. Mildred was actually an ordained minister and provided help with some of the mailroom duties. Bob was very handy with maintenance needs that came up. Their heart's passion, however, was sharing the love of Christ with the Navajos living on the reservation land.

Many of the Navajos at that time had no running water or electricity in their homes. A small barrel with a smokestack reaching through the roof of an eight sided log hogan was a source of heat and also served as a cookstove in their primitive dirt-floored homes. The Sharples loved to spend time with these families, providing clothes and food. During their visits they also shared Christ's love and led many to Jesus as their savior.

When the winter weather brought snow and rain, the dirt roads that led to rutted trails became impassable to these remote homes. While we thought that the Love Dove plane would help us get supplies to these remote areas, we began to realize that rising insurance costs and excessive maintenance costs were becoming a burden. About that time we heard of a ministry in Texas that needed a plane to stay in constant communication with their Bible students in Mexico and Central America.

So, we sold the plane to them and used those funds to purchase a new four-wheel-drive vehicle appropriately named, "Trail Duster." Not long after the purchase, the Sharples visited a family 20 miles off the main road through deep mud to a home where they led a Navajo couple to the Lord. The Trail Duster went where the Love Dove could have never gone. We traded our wings for wheels, which continued to provide reliable transportation for these impactful visits for many years to come.

As spring came to a close, heavy equipment came onto the grounds. Before construction could begin on the new Communication Center it was necessary to replace our old sewer line with a new one that would handle the increased activity of this new building and others that would come later.

As we prayed together as a family in our evening devotions we had been sharing a verse from Psalm 127:1 with the kids that I had been using regularly when talking with people about our new building project. "Unless the Lord builds the house, its builders labor in vain ... " When 3-year-old Byron looked out the window and saw all those "big diggers" crawling off the trailers, he went running to Kay and said, "Mommy, mom ... God is out there building our building!"

I couldn't help but think, "You're right Byron. God *is* out there building our building." He was doing it through the hands of His people who donated dollars for the project. And, he was building through the hands of those who volunteered in one way or another. One of those volunteers owned the earth moving equipment that just arrived. While we didn't ask for the work to be donated, that's exactly what happened. It was a major job which required the ditch to be 17 feet deep at the city street, but this man knew there was another verse in Psalm 127:3 (NLT) that reflected the value that God placed on His children – "Children are a gift from God; they are His reward."

A few months later more good news came our way. After a wearisome, prolonged wait, on August 3rd the Federal Communications Commission issued Navajo Missions Inc. a permit for construction of an educational non-commercial Christian radio station! This was the final barrier in moving ahead with the actual installation of equipment and construction of this first Christian radio station in the Four Corners area.

All broadcast stations west of the Mississippi began their call letters with K plus three more letters. We requested the additional letters NMI which stood for Navajo Missions Inc. One of our hold-ups was the fact that KNMI was previously assigned to a seagoing ship that was now out of commission. The FCC finally was able to recall those letters and issue them to us. With this permit we were able to physically begin to construct the sound-proof walls on two rooms in the corner of our maintenance shop which would be the temporary home of the station until the new Communication Center was completed.

Even with this good news we still faced the challenge of raising an additional $26,000. We didn't know how or when, but we knew that the same God who placed this challenge to broadcast in our hearts would be faithful in bringing it to pass. It was just a few weeks later when a middle-aged Navajo lady came into our bookstore. She spoke only Navajo and with the help of her daughter asked how to make out a check for the new Communication Center. Imagine the surprise of our sales clerk when she saw the gift was $5,000! We didn't know this lady and she had never given to us before. We did find out that she had received a large amount of money through some gas leases and wanted to share this gift to help her own people. Truly, God *does* speak Navajo.

Sunday, March 16, 1980 was definitely a RED LETTER day at Navajo Missions. It was the day that we put KNMI, the first Christian radio station in the Four Corners area, on the air! At 2 p.m. we gathered together with board members and others along with Farmington Mayor Bob Culpepper for a ribbon-cutting ceremony at the transmitter building next to the local TV tower on the bluffs. General Manager of the station, Mark Frederick, and Pete Parise, our new operations and engineer staff member, held both ends of the ribbon with Jack Drake and the Mayor holding the large scissors that officially cut loose Christian programming to the airwaves.

With the power turned on to the transmitter, we scurried down the winding road that led to the Mission and our small studios on West Main Street. Jack voiced the first words heard on the air which included a scripture and a prayer. A Navajo man living 30 miles away in Shiprock heard the dedication ceremonies over the air. Although he was sick in bed he told his wife, "We got to go help Jack celebrate this special day." He and many others came and went during that first afternoon sharing their testimonies, often in Navajo.

While the power of the station was only 410 watts, the FM frequency would reach Farmington and beyond into the Four Corners area. In the future we planned to add FM translators in other areas that would boost our signal into more far reaching communities. Our broadcast day was 6 a.m. to 7 p.m. seven days a week. On our first Monday a man called in with a prayer request looking for a job. A few minutes later another man called to say, "I have a job for that previous caller." The connections were being made. God was beginning to use this station to dramatically change the air waves for years to come.

Most of our broadcast day was in English, but from 1-3 p.m. each weekday, Andy Begay, a full-blooded Navajo evangelist hosted our Navajo language programming. Andy had once done interpreting for Billy Graham when he was in Albuquerque. During his show time he would use his Native tongue between the songs to encourage and point our Navajo listeners to Jesus. There were Navajo teaching programs, including David Tutt, a Navajo Bible translator, who had a 15- minute program that taught Navajos to read and write their language. (Many who speak the language can't read or write it). While there weren't many music recordings in Navajo, many of the Navajo listeners enjoyed Southern Gospel music, which was featured during these hours.

The morning programming included inspiration-al-style Christian music mixed in with Christian Talk shows like J. Vernon McGee, Back to the Bible, Focus on the Family, Kenneth Copeland and others. We also had a Prayer and Praise time when listeners would call in their requests.

From 4-5 p.m. each weekday, I co-hosted a show with Mark Frederick, and then with Johnny Creasong, and then with Pat Wells, called "The Going Home Show." It was a variety of music, interviews and fun including Bible Baseball games along with news and views of the day. I also had a short 5-minute recorded program called "Joyful Gems from Jim" that featured humorous thoughts and anecdotes mixed with catchy one-liners that would hopefully put a smile on faces and brighten their days.

The next couple of hours that led up to the close of our broadcast day at 7 p.m. featured more contemporary Christian music for the younger generation. While the teens and young adults enjoyed the new artists with their up-beat style, the older adults let us know that they didn't approve. Some even accused us of playing "the devil's music." Being the only Christian station in the area, we were trying to provide programming that the entire family, including various cultures, could enjoy.

We soon discovered that we would always have some who would not approve of the mix of music and even Bible teaching styles. Jack Drake helped to quiet the frustrations of those who were in his age group when he shared this example. He said, "When I go fishing I use worms for bait to catch the fish. I don't like the worms, but the fish do so I will use them to catch fish. In the same way, I may not like the sound of the music that our young people are listening to, but if we can use the songs of these Christian artists to reach our youth with a positive message then I'm willing to do so."

The excitement and life-changing potential of Christian radio … this was what I envisioned back in Pennsylvania several years earlier. It wasn't meant to be then or there, but now God had used me to bring this dream to Navajoland in Farmington, New Mexico and I couldn't have been happier.

My days were also spent doing what made me the happiest—being a mother. I felt so blessed to have the two-fold joy of loving, nurturing and planting God's Word into the lives of my own two children, Lisa and David, as well as into the lives of the children God continued to bring into our care. Our family always consisted of several infants and toddlers. It also meant some very humorous moments in the life of our family.

In the first couple of years when David and Byron were babies, our two oldest girls would race to the van when it was time to go to church, or some other activity. Their favorite trick was to grab one of the boys and hide him in the back seat of the van, hoping to make us think we had forgotten one of them. I was used to counting heads whenever we left home, or any other location, so it was a real challenge for the girls to trick us.

There was one Sunday, however, when we were running late and heading off to church in a frenzy. This was before the days of mandatory car seats, so I was holding David (only a couple months old) on my lap. A quick head count and we were off to church. A half mile away from home, the girls began their game by saying, "Where's Byron – we don't have Byron." I played along with them, as I usually did, knowing they had him in the back seat. Moments later, David soiled his diaper, causing diarrhea to fill his diaper and run out onto my skirt. As we headed back to the house to change clothes, the girls continued to ask about Byron.

We arrived back at the Mission and I carried David into the house – but not before I walked along the side of the van, looking in windows and checking the back seat. Sure enough, Genevieve and Caroline sat in the backseat – without Byron. Jim and I, and nine kids, nearly knocked each other over trying to get into the house and look for Byron. A frantic search found nine- month-old Byron had crawled to the far end of the house and into our bathroom. He was sitting in the middle of the floor, and I'm convinced he was trying to process the new sound he was hearing after we had all left – silence!

Another time we were taking our children to Pennsylvania for vacation. Each time we left the van and entered again, we counted heads. One late afternoon, after driving three hours, we stopped for supper. Some of the children had been sleeping, so pillows were thrown aside as children made their way out of the van. When our headcount produced nine children instead of 10, Jim and I looked at each other and counted again. I was so panicked; I couldn't even think what child was missing or where we had last stopped. Leaping into the van, Jim began tossing pillows, books, and toys that littered the van floor. Lying sound asleep under the last van seat, covered with pillows, was five-year-old Pauline. As Jim and I caught our breath and hugged Pauline, we were reminded again of the wisdom, tenacity, and Godly grace needed to successfully care for a "Bakers' Dozen."

Then and now, we often thank God for the protection He gave us over the thousands of miles we traveled with our children. We were privileged to show children in our care the joy of lightning bugs in Pennsylvania, a Passion Play in South Dakota, tourist attractions such as Dodge City and Balboa Island, along with amusement parks in

Texas, California, Pennsylvania, and Colorado. We shared history with them as we visited Gettysburg, the Liberty Bell, and even stood outside the doorway of the Oval Office at the nation's capitol with my brother and three of our older children. We wondered, at the time, if the children would ever appreciate this extremely rare opportunity they were experiencing.

One vacation took us to Mt. Rushmore, where we spent a very memorable evening. It was cloudy when we arrived, late in the afternoon. While sitting in front of the monument, waiting for the evening lights to come on, we experienced a downpour. We all raced to a nearby tree to take cover. Waiting out the rain, we returned to the monument, just as the lights were coming on. The entire crowd began to laugh as we viewed the four presidents. The space under their noses had remained dry, while the other areas of their faces were wet from rain. All four presidents looked like they had runny noses. Returning to our van, we realized the battery had died and we were stranded in the parking lot. Our children spent the next couple of hours singing songs, telling stories and eating everything in the van as we waited for a mechanic to arrive and get us up and running again.

From the New Jersey shore to the Pacific Ocean, our years of traveling with our children provided not only them, but us, with memories that continue to bring us great joy. Repeatedly, we have seen some of our children return as adults, with their spouses and/or children, and ask us to show them the pictures we took of them on vacation. We have also seen how God, in His faithfulness, has blessed the growth of the Mission, not only in buildings, but, more importantly, through the lives of the children who called Navajo Missions their home.

Chapter Thirteen

TRANSFORMATIONS

The early 1980s brought on busy days as we strived to secure the funding necessary to provide for the ongoing needs of KNMI radio. We were not a commercial station so we had to rely on the support of local listeners. Some of those were business owners, too, so we were able to provide grant announcements thanking them for their support. We continued to operate the station from the corner of the maintenance shop while construction continued on the new Communication Center.

It was quite amusing to have guests come to share on the radio and have to lead them around table saws, tools and supplies, back the narrow hallway to the small studio and control room. It was a regular occurrence to shout out the door to the maintenance men, "Turn off the saws, guys ... we're going live." On one of those visits, Grady Nutt, known as "America's Prime Minister of Humor," came for a concert at the Civic Center. Those who are old enough will remember he was the minister featured on the "Hee Haw" TV Show. As he walked through the shop he picked up a broom and shouted, "Do you use this to clean out the grooves in the albums?"

Other Christian artists came to Farmington to perform concerts at our local Civic Center, which seated 1,200 people. Dave Boyer, The Cruse Family, Dino, Don Francisco and Doug Oldham were some who came to help us raise funds for KNMI. Doug was physically ill when he stepped off the plane that provided a rough ride over the Rockies to Farmington. "Whew!" he said as he mopped his brow, shaking his head. And, with that, he was off for a quick visit of the Mission prior to the evening concert.

That night Doug began singing as he sat in one of the seats in the auditorium, "Where the Spirit of the Lord is, there is peace ... " "Do you believe that?" he asked the crowd. "Then keep it on the air. Let the Spirit of the Lord permeate your city. Let Him reach out and touch lives! I believe that one day KNMI will reach more people in one day than the Master was able to speak to in His whole time on earth!" Those words were prophetic as three decades later this station would not only broadcast to the people of the Four Corners area but to the people of the four corners of the world through live streaming on the Internet.

During the intermission break of Doug Oldham's concert, a local song writer and singer, Ronna Jordan, was able to share a few of her songs from her first album. One of the songs she sang that night was inspired by a story she heard on KNMI. One of the programs we aired each morning was "Focus on the Family," hosted by Dr. James Dobson. He told the story of a 5-year-old boy who was in the hospital dying of lung cancer.

Nurses kept hearing the boy talking about hearing bells. The head nurse told his mother he was hallucinating. His mother said, "No, I told him whenever it hurts, or he is frightened, to think of the bells of heaven ringing there in the corner of his room." The boy went to heaven hearing those bells. After hearing this story, Ronna was inspired to write a song about this boy and also honor a local teenager named Todd who was critically ill. He passed away while she was in Nashville recording her first album that included the song, "Don't Cry Mama."

Doug was so impressed with Ronna's anointing that night that he chose one of her songs, "Smack Dab in the Middle" to perform and record, himself. Dr. Dobson also showed interest in using "Don't Cry Mama" in a new telecast he was preparing at the time. Ronna said, "All of this because I tuned into KNMI." The next three days we held the first Share-A-Thon for the station. Many great testimonies were called in from listeners, along with monthly commitments of nearly $4,000. This was a great start for what would become a vibrant broadcast ministry that would touch many lives over the years.

During the summer of 1981, it was time to pack up the van and take all the kids back to Lancaster Pennsylvania for vacation. We left Lisa's long-haired dachshund, Gretel, in the care of a local family, Bob and Leslie Fitz. Their daughter, Jana, went to school with Lisa and they had become good friends. Being dog lovers and owners, we knew Gretel would be in safe hands. The Fitzs picked up Gretel the day before we were to leave for Pennsylvania, and headed to the Colorado mountains for the weekend. An hour after their departure from our home, the phone rang. Gretel had run off when they let her out of the van for a potty break. She was roaming the hills at the Colorado border and could not be found.

Thinking Gretel would come to us if she heard familiar voices, I loaded the kids in the van and headed to where Bob and Leslie were waiting for us. We called and called, but there was no sign of Gretel. We left Bob's business cards with the local residents, who warned us of coyotes and other larger animals who would find a small dog to be fair prey. With sad hearts, we headed back to Farmington, while Bob and Leslie continued on to Colorado. Lisa held her tears until after we left Bob and Leslie, but they flowed non-stop the whole way back to Farmington.

Entering our home, Lisa ran to her room and found solace on her bed with her favorite blanket. Within minutes, Jack Drake was at our door. In the midst of his busy day, Jack always found time to pray with those in need. Today was no exception. He asked if he could pray with Lisa and I led him to her room. I will never forget this caring man laying his hand on Lisa's head and praying for the return of her beloved pet. His prayer had a calming effect on all of us and his example served as a reminder to me over the years that nothing is too small to take to God in prayer.

We left the next day for Pennsylvania, as planned. During the next couple of days, Mark Frederick would drive to the Colorado border, looking for Gretel. One time he spotted her sitting in the middle of the road. When he stopped to call her to the car, Gretel headed for the hills again. Our second night on the road, we were staying in Kansas. We receive a call from Jack saying Gretel was safely home. Some oil field workers had given her fresh water and food each day and had slowly lured her to their truck, rescuing her from her three-day adventure. Laughingly, Jack told us Gretel wanted to "talk to Lisa." He put the dog to the phone and she barked excitedly when she heard Lisa's voice. This time Lisa would shed tears of joy!

These trips were always an adventure as we spoke in various states, representing the mission in church services. On this particular trip, we included Cindy, our secretary who lived in our home, and Judy, one of the Navajo teens who had just graduated and wanted to visit a potential college in Ohio.

I really admire Jim's and my parents as they opened their doors to 14 of us. We were quite a houseful that summer. One hot, humid day, we were in my parents' living room, sorting out Navajo skirts, shirts and pants, preparing for an evening service. My dad sat in his chair, watching all the organized chaos that came with getting 10 kids dressed, hair done etc. In the midst of the commotion, Dad quietly asked, "Kate, do you think you found your nitch in life?" It was one of those defining moments as I paused briefly to consider the question. I had to admit this large family, though noisy, busy and a source of a lot of work, gave me a great sense of purpose and joy. It truly was "my nitch" and there was nothing else I wanted to do with my life.

This particular trip had some frustrating moments, too. The first weekend in Pennsylvania, I joined my siblings and our children for a softball game at the ball field of the elementary school that I once attended. As I ran for a fly ball I stepped into a suppressed area of the field and heard the snap and crack of my leg as I fell to the ground. So, I was taken off to the emergency room of the local hospital.

Little did I know at the time that there was a crisis occurring with the emergency staff. Three emergency workers were called to the scene of an abandoned septic tank. An 8-year-old boy had been emptying clippings into the tank when he dropped a grass-catcher from a mower into it. He climbed down to retrieve it and was overcome by methane gas. The three emergency workers died trying to save the boy–who was safely removed, but suffered brain injuries. I didn't learn of their emergency until four hours later when they finally took me back to confirm my broken leg.

On our return trip to Farmington, our travels took us through St. Louis. We were blessed with friends and supporters along the way who would allow us to throw out sleeping bags on the floor, which saved us lots of money on lodging. Sometimes we would make use of the "Mennonite your Way" program where Christian families would list their names in the directory indicating that fellow Christians could spend the night in their home for a nominal per-person amount.

We would often get silence on the other end of the phone when making the contact saying that there were 12 of us in our family. Surprisingly, there were those who agreed to our arrival.. One of those was a pastor in St. Louis. As I left the freeway and maneuvered through the hot city streets, we ended up at the pastor's daughter's apartment, where we had been instructed to call him for our final directions.

As Kay and I stood at her doorway we looked around at the surroundings. High-rise, low-rent apartment buildings with unscreened windows allowed the curtains to flutter in and out as residents took notice of these strangers in their midst. And, we must have been quite the site to behold. I was on crutches. Our niece, Con Maser, was returning from Pennsylvania with us and she also was on crutches following foot surgery. Our van was loaded with kids. A car-top carrier was on the roof with all the extra stuff we couldn't jam under the seats.

Standing at the front door of the apartment, I placed the call to the pastor. Someone else answered and asked us to wait a minute. After five minutes of waiting, this person returned to the phone to say that the pastor would be delayed in coming to the phone because someone had just shot out the window to his car! As Kay and I looked at each other, we didn't need to say a word. We knew it was time to go. Two blocks away, as we found our way through this ghetto-ridden part of the city, we noticed the yellow tape that accompanies police activity at a crime scene. The city playground was surrounded by tape and people. There were burly looking guys walking about with baseball bats and there wasn't a ball field in sight.

What a relief it was to finally make our way back to Interstate 70, headed west out of St. Louis. We drove for an hour before pulling into a modest motel in the countryside. We got two adjoining rooms and ordered a couple of pizzas from a nearby pizza shop. We were finally able to relax, reflecting on another day with the Bakers' dozen. As we watched the 10 p.m. news from St. Louis we noticed that the lead story showed the same yellow-taped playground that we had driven by earlier in the evening. You guessed it. It was the scene of a murder. As we joined our family together for prayer that night, we thanked God for his protection, a safe place to sleep and provision for the pastor and his family as he ministered to those living in the inner city. We were thankful that God had called us to our Navajo neighbors nearly 1,000 miles west of St. Louis, the Gateway to the West.

It was 3:30 a.m. on March 26, 1982 when Mark Frederick called me on the intercom. "Jim, I've already called the Fire Department. The barn is on fire!" I quickly threw on some clothes and ran to the front door. Three of our homes for children were silhouetted by the orange glow of the inferno that had flames shooting into the trees. I instinctively grabbed my camera on the way out the door knowing I would need to send a letter to our mission friends telling them of our need to rebuild our barn. And, a picture is worth a thousand words. We lost 1,000 bales of hay and some small animals that night. We never found out for sure what caused the fire, but it could have been spontaneous combustion.

A few weeks later we had *spontaneous cooperation* from dozens of friends in the community. Being from Amish country in Pennsylvania, I knew how the Amish folks would come together and rebuild a barn in one day! I wondered if something like that could happen in Farmington. Thanks to the coordination of our builder friend, Bill Anglin, we gathered a few dozen people together on Easter weekend for an old-fashioned barn raisin'. The men bored holes for posts, cement was poured and framework came together like time-lapse photography of a flower unfolding. How exciting these days were as we saw God turn a tragedy into a triumph!

Amid joyful chatter, some ladies whipped up hearty meals of spaghetti and frybread. (After all we are in Navajo country, so you have to have frybread). Like ants, the workers teamed together and hammered away. Dick Ullrich, our Chairman of the Board, actually carried many of the boards to the carpenters that day. Mark Frederick, General Manager of KNMI, put up a large speaker that provided great Christian music from KNMI throughout the two days. I was humbled, yet elated, as the community of Christ came together, helping us restore the barn to one that was bigger and better than the original one. In an effort to provide a bit of humor as I expressed our deep gratitude to the community, I put this message on the sign in front of our Communication Center: THANKS TO OUR MANY FRIENDS WE HAVE HAD A REAL BARN – AGAIN EXPERIENCE.

A year later, it was April 10, 1983. Hard to believe eight years had passed since we drove onto the Mission grounds on that date in 1975. This April 10th was special also. After five years of planning, praying, fund raising, more praying and building, the Communication Center was being dedicated to God's glory. There had been so many times when this project stalled, due to lack of funding, and our faith was tested.

For nearly a year and a half the concrete walls had stood alone through winter snows and summer sun. But sometimes when we least expected it, God's faithfulness would become evident as He moved in the hearts of His people and funds would be given to continue construction again. We were learning God's plans are flawless and He would see the completion of this building in His perfect timing. God also provided volunteers to come and help with the construction. While we didn't have the entire five-level Center completed, we were able to move into the offices, including the much-needed new studios for KNMI on the upper level. Our one-time playground was now transformed into a beautiful building that would enable our staff to continue the various areas of ministry in an efficient way.

I shared these words at the dedication service, "When we first got the vision from the Lord for this Center, we asked the Lord to give us a verse of scripture that would sustain us through the construction of this building. He gave us Habakkuk 2:3 (NLT). "But these things I plan won't happen right away. Slowly, steadily, surely, the time approaches when the vision will be fulfilled. If it seems slow, wait patiently, for it will surely take place. It will not be delayed." Over the years I would have many more times to remember these comforting words.

Over 300 people crowded into the lobby of the center. Some gathered on the upper level taking in the festivities from above. The overflow crowd spilled out the front doors and many more listened to the live broadcast on KNMI. Founder Jack Drake said, "I believe God has great things in store for us. However, let's remember that though we appreciate this building and praise God for it, we are not worshipping it. It is simply a facility, an instrument. We're really talking about a building of people that is alive ... the Body of Christ, and the builder is the Lord Jesus Christ!"

There were many who made this day special. Soloists, a Navajo choir, city and state leaders and one of the first children taken into the mission 30 years earlier, Mary Clugston. She grew up at the Mission, went on to higher education and served on the President's National Commission on Education in Washington. As the program of dedication came to a close, Rev. Johnny Creasong, a local pastor and Music Director for KNMI, led those in attendance with an appropriate chorus: "There's a sweet,

sweet spirit in this place. And I know that it's the Spirit of the Lord ... " There are sweet expressions on each face ... " It had been a wonderful, happy day.

What a joy it had been to see God's transformation take place throughout this ministry. The birth of KNMI in the corner of a garage was being transformed into a powerful ministry that was impacting lives throughout the Four Corners region. People were getting saved, delivered and encouraged in their walk with Christ. Kay and I were seeing children accept Christ in our home. Many destitute Navajo families were dramatically blessed through the reservation ministry. Even the old barn was transformed into a new one after the devastating fire. And, the open lot in the central part of our property was now the focal point of our various ministries, appropriately named the Communication Center.

Speaking of communication, it was about this time God sent us a talented lady named Ollive Iles. At one time, Ollive worked for the old Bell Telephone Company as a switchboard operator. While we didn't need her to plug lines into a switchboard, we did need someone to communicate our mission goals and objectives by phone and mail to our current and prospective donors across the nation. Ollive's friendly personality made her a natural at building relationships and friendships with those who had a vision to help Navajo Missions, or learn more about the ministries taking place. Before long, Ollive became our first Director of Development and was a great asset to me as we continued to expand and develop new sources of income for the growing ministry. Her wise counsel and love for the Lord would be such a blessing to this ministry for nearly 20 years.

Ollive contacted a couple of long-time donors of the Mission to ask if they would like to become field representatives for Navajo Missions. One of the first volunteers to sign up as a field representative was Sandra Pobanz. Sandra began supporting the Mission in 1974. It was through her parents and church in Geneseo, Illinois that the first connection was made. Kay and I, along with Joe and Gerri Begay, had several opportunities to share the work of the Mission at this church when we traveled in the Midwest. One time Sandra even coordinated a Navajo Taco Supper at the church. Joe and Gerri did their best to make nearly 75 pieces of fry bread for the crowd that gathered. As a respresentative, Sandra did a great job in presenting the Mission to churches, schools and Sunday School Conventions.

After relocating in Scottsdale, Arizona in October 2010, Sandra joined our Board of Directors. More recently, Sandra has become President of the separate Navajo Heritage Museum Board, which is beginning to raise funds for a museum on the Ministry campus that will highlight the history and culture of the Navajo people. Sandra is just one example of many friends who have volunteered their services over the years.

In the midst of all the exciting happenings at the Mission there was one transformation taking place that broke our hearts. With now close to 10 years of ministry, we were beginning to see the tremendous toll our years as houseparents were taking on our own two children. Although Lisa seemed to enjoy the busy pace of a large family, David seemed to get stuck in the grief of having children come and go in and out of his young life. Having moved to New Mexico at 3, Lisa's first years of life had provided her with a sense of belonging, both to us and to her extended family of grandparents, aunts, uncles and cousins living in Pennsylvania. Having lived at Navajo Missions since birth, Dave did not have the advantage of living with his parents without other children in the home.

One day, as several natural parents came to check out their children for the weekend, David threw himself on our couch and cried, "When will my real mother and father come to check me out?" My heart broke as I realized my failure in helping David to know his rightful place as our son. We had tried so hard to help our Navajo children experience a strong sense of family life and had failed to give David his needed sense of belonging to Jim and me in a way our Navajo children could never experience. We made immediate plans to take Lisa and David on their first vacation without our Navajo children as soon as the opportunity was available. It was our hope that this time spent with his small, natural family would give Dave a visual picture of who his biological family was and help him in the identity crises he was experiencing.

We also sought the help of a local counselor. David was struggling in school, at home, and in his heart. The counselor's advice was three-fold: Find a smaller school for David where he would get more individual help and could experience more success, make more time for David to spend with his dad, and leave our role as houseparents.

We were not prepared for the spiritual battle that would take place in the months ahead as we absorbed the suggestions given us. We were immediately able to find a small Christian school that was able to meet David's needs. Jim made more time to be with David on an individual basis. But leaving our positions as houseparents was something we struggled with on a daily basis.

I would lie in bed at night and plead with God to allow me to hear His direction for a change in my responsibilities. I knew I had heard His call to come to Navajo Missions as a housemother, and I knew I would know His voice if He would tell me to leave. We weighed the option of moving off the Mission grounds, find housing in town and letting Jim continue in leadership at the Mission. It seemed like a reasonable way to be able to devote more of my time to David and Lisa and still continue to be a part of the ministry we were called to 10 years ago.

Weeks passed, then months, and our struggle continued. For the second time in our lives, we found ourselves counting the cost of following God's call. Ten years prior, when we first felt called to Navajo Missions, we naively focused on what it would cost Jim and me. Now, we were finding we were reconsidering our commitment based upon what it would cost our children.

We found no peace in our hearts when we thought about leaving, but there was no peace in our hearts by staying either. What would lie ahead for our son and daughter if we decided to stay on as houseparents? What toll would it take on our children and how would David survive the sadness and grief he seemed to be experiencing? These questions kept Jim and me awake at night, and drained our energy during the day. We needed to hear from the Lord and know His peace again.

As I poured over the scriptures, I searched for answers. I related to Abraham and the pain and questions he surely faced as he placed his son on the altar. I had read enough stories written by MKs (missionary kids) to know their lives did not all have happy endings without emotional scars. While in our hearts all we wanted to do was relieve David's pain and sadness, God was asking us to trust Him with David's life and stay on the course He had set before us.

He reminded me of the pain Mary experienced at the cost of her Son, Jesus, going to the cross out of obedience to His Father. Jesus' perfect love for his mother did not keep Him from fulfilling God's plan for His life, thereby providing for our salvation. Jim and I were beginning to see our intense love for our children had to be secondary to our love for Christ. We understood the commitment God was again asking us to make, but we found it much harder this time to follow His call than it was 10 years earlier.

God also spoke to us through an article that was published by our Churches of God denomination. The article was entitled "God Chooses Well." My spirit found hope when I read, "In 'Who's Who' and the 'Hall of Fame' there are more sons and daughters from men of the ministry than from men of any other single profession. If you are born a child of a minister, your chances at success are 25 times greater than if you are born a child of any other professional person. The only parents to surpass the ministers in this respect are the missionaries."

When we finally made the decision to stay as houseparents, and trust the Lord for the outcome, God's peace settled on our lives. We claimed the promise of (Galations 6:9) "Let us not become weary in doing good, for at the proper time we will reap a harvest if we do not give up."

Although our children still had struggles during the following years, we saw God's hand of protection rest upon them as He walked through each experience with them. Their experiences would make them into the fine adults they would become in the future.

I once read, "It is a good thing to have no troubles. But it is a far greater thing to have troubles and find the grace to walk through them." As our small family entered the stormy years of Lisa and David's teen years, God would provide the love and grace to walk through each trial. My faith was often weak, even to the point of questioning God's willingness to keep our family in the hollow of His hand. Some of the struggles broke Jim and me as parents, seeing our failures and the way they affected David and Lisa. But the struggles also gave us new insight into God's unconditional love for His children and His willingness to transform the lives of anyone who would seek His will and plan. We thank God for His forgiveness, His loving discipline and His amazing grace. Great is His faithfulness!

Chapter Fourteen

A DYNAMIC DECADE

As we moved into our second decade of service at the mission, it became more evident to me that my primary focus was not going to remain with the position of houseparent. Jack was becoming more and more dependent on my leadership as I became more of the new face of Navajo Missions. In celebration of Jack's 30 years of ministry, we hosted a banquet at the Civic Center attended by a few hundred admirers and supporters. We provided Jack and Betty with a trip to Israel, which they thoroughly enjoyed.

These years were fascinating as we saw the ministry growing. New staff was replacing some of the "old-timers." Mark and Karen Frederick were very committed as houseparents and, of course, Mark was operating the radio station, too. Karen even did some D.J. work on occasion. She also knew some Spanish, which was helpful at times; especially the year that we hosted six ball players from Puerto Rico who were here for the annual Connie Mack World Series.

By now, Lisa's relationship with her friend, Jana, was growing. Jana's friendship provided Lisa with a place to visit that wasn't connected with the Mission. Through the loss (and rescue) of Gretel, Leslie's and my relationship grew, too. She opened her home and heart to me and, I enjoyed having a friendship that wasn't connected to Navajo Missions. Until ...

Leslie and her husband, Bob, had adopted a little boy, Chris, and they were talking about adopting another child. I joked with Leslie and said, "Don't adopt another child. Come to Navajo Missions and we'll give you 10 kids! The seed was planted and before long, we were meeting with Bob and Leslie concerning an opening we had for houseparents and a business manager. Unbeknown to us, Bob had a background in business and was a perfect fit for the available position. With a straight face, Bob asked us, "What would I do in my spare time besides being a housedad and keeping books?"

Bob and Leslie came to the Mission for a tour of the facilities and to continue their interview process with us. God was working in their hearts, but He gave them an extra nudge the day they came for their final interview with our Chairman of the Board. Before their arrival, Jim had picked up the Mission mail at the post office and was sorting it into the individual boxes of those who lived on the Mission grounds. Imagine his surprise when he found a new edition of the New Wine Magazine, addressed to Bob and Leslie at their current Farmington address. Only God could have arranged that mistake. When Bob and Leslie arrived for their visit, Jim laughingly said, "You might as well move here, Bob, because your mail has already begun arriving at our Mission mailbox." Bob was soon to find out what he would do in his "spare" time. He *and Leslie joined our staff on June 1, 1982. They imme- diately became houseparents to seven Navajo children, in addition to their own three children.*

Bob and Leslie Fitz became solid members of our houseparent staff and a natural fit with the existing staff. Leslie quickly spiced up the friendship Karen and I had developed, making our fellowship times a threesome. Bob's expertise in accounting and business provided the needed depth in that department as he performed those services in conjunction with being a housedad. Within a short time, John and Diane Ritter, local friends of the ministry, heard of our need for houseparents and joined our team. John was an expert in maintenance and he pro- vided many improvements during the time he and Diane served at the Mission.

Jim and I felt like we had received an extra portion of grace from the Lord as He brought these two couples to serve with the Fredericks and us. Since our arrival, we had never enjoyed such great camaraderie among the four houseparent couples who served in the homes. We enjoyed working together, laughing together and even crying together. We were our own support group and the strength Jim and I received through the friend- ships and teamwork of these three other couples gave us a renewed vision for our work as houseparents – just when we needed it!

Our team continued to change with Bessie Largo becoming our cook. She had worked with Jack back in the early 1950s when he lived in Burnham, a small community in the Navajo Nation about 30 miles south of Farmington. She had served as cook previously at a government boarding school before her early retirement. As a Navajo, Bessie was a wonderful role model to the children, providing all of them with unconditional love and direction. She shared her wisdom and insight with us as houseparents, helping us to understand some of the background and culture of the children we cared for each day. Bessie fed us physically, as well as spiritually, as she consistently shared her love for Christ. She kept her Bible by the kitchen door, witnessing faithfully to those who came off the street wanting a bite to eat. We were fortunate to have her serve as cook for eight years, until she retired for the second time. We put together some of her favorite recipes in a booklet called *Bessie's Best Navajo Recipes*.

Art and Louise Hickmott were aunt and uncle to the Fredericks, having lived for many years in Michigan, where Art worked in the auto industry. After visiting here, they believed that God was calling them to join our staff. I responded to their letter saying that we didn't have a need at that time. But, they were persistent and packed their lives into a van with a large trailer behind and made their way to Farmington, anyway.

Within a short time of their arrival, we wondered how we ever got along without them. Louise quickly put her organizational skills into action as she ran our mailing room in a very efficient way. Hickmotts became "Aunt Louise and Uncle Art" to all the children who lived on grounds. Art fixed countless flat tires on bicycles for hundreds of children. He could fix any vehicle and worked on motors of any kind. Continuing his work at Navajo Missions long after Aunt Louise passed away, he was a reliable maintenance man and endearing friend to both children and staff. We were all deeply saddened when he passed away on September 9, 2013.

Bob and Mildred Sharples were another dear couple that backed their 29-foot-long camper in next to our shop building. They had a heart to serve and just wanted to minister to the Navajo people in our region. They quickly became our "adopted parents" eating holiday meals with us and faithfully watching the Olympics with us every four years. We always looked forward to Mildred's famous cherry cheesecake desserts. Mildred spent her first six years supervising the mailroom. Bob was a well-rounded maintenance man, especially good with plumbing and woodworking. Their last four years of ministry was spent serving with our Navajo Nation Outreach, visiting in the homes of families who were experiencing physical and spiritual needs.

A similar experience took place with Larry and Evelyn McNickle, who arrived one day from Pennsylvania along with their adult children in a converted school bus. They wanted to visit the Mission and see what God was doing. I immediately felt a connection with Evelyn and felt like I knew her. She looked very much like my mother and I couldn't shake the feeling I had seen her before. Larry, Evelyn, and their son and daughter ate supper with us in our home. Later that evening, they went with us to Bible Study in one of the other homes. It was during that time they shared their testimonies and Evelyn mentioned the years she and Larry served as camp counselors at Doubling Gap Church of God Camp in the mountains of central Pennsylvania. Immediately I knew where I had met her. When we arrived back at our house, I dug out my camp pictures. There I was, a skinny 10-year-old, standing with my camp counselor – Evelyn McNickle.

It was amazing how God wove His team together. Eventually, the McNickles moved to the Mission and spent many years ministering to disadvantaged Navajo families living in remote areas of the Navajo Nation. While the moms and elderly grandparents were looking through the boxes of used clothing in the back of the four-wheel drive vehicle, Larry and Evelyn became friends, Navajo neighbors, with those who were once strangers. Prayers were offered, some got involved in Bible studies with them, and many accepted Christ as their Savior.

As the need arose for new missionaries to serve with us in various areas of the ministry, God would bring us just the right people at the right time with the talents and abilities that He knew would benefit our outreach. Homer and Mary Lou Stepanek, long-time farmers from Missouri joined our staff. While they were quite an asset to our small farm program at the Mission, they came with a desire to share Christ's love with the Navajos living in remote areas of the Navajo Nation, just west of the Farmington area. Homer and Mary Lou loved and nurtured everyone they met. They had hearts of devotion for the Lord and love just spilled out of their lives unto children and adults alike. The Stepaneks were a blessing to many and committed missionaries with us until their retirement. They continue to be loyal friends to this ministry.

In the fall of 1984, I arranged a speaking trip for Jack that included church services and a banquet in our home town of Lancaster. While Jack often traveled the country to share the work of Navajo Missions, he hadn't been to this area. I felt it was important for him to connect with our family and friends who supported us in such a generous way. Jack wanted someone to travel with him for this extended four-week trip. That's when we first met Joe and Gerri Begay. Joe agreed to spend the month on the road with Jack. He was the highlight of their visits and presentations. Everybody wanted to meet this Indian man from Navajoland.

Joe and Gerri were a delightful Navajo couple who had experienced God's amazing grace in their lives. They willingly shared their miraculous story of God's compassionate mercy and forgiveness. Being once bound by alcohol, bitterness and unfaithfulness, their broken lives had experienced two divorces ... from each other! But, then God came into their midst and reconciliation took place. They found peace with God and each other. Before long they were married a third time to each other. And, now they believed God was calling them into some kind of ministry. And, wow ... what an amazing ministry they continue to have, bringing a message of hope to hurting souls across the nation and especially the Navajo Nation.

Little did we know then that Joe and Gerri would become our dearest friends and fellow missionaries, travelling with us to nearly every state over the next 30 years. As we traveled thousands of miles together over the years, our hearts connected as we shared joys and sorrows, victories and defeats. We prayed together and sang together. We would often begin our day of travel with a devotion, followed by a prayer for our safety, protection and divine appointments for the day.

Joe and Gerri's love for others was evident as we ministered together in churches, visited in schools and homes and conducted radio and television interviews. The Begays appeared on "The 700 Club" and had their testimony dramatized on the popular radio show, "Unshackled," produced by Pacific Garden Mission in Chicago. Their testimony is also featured in "The Conquering Indian," a book compiled by Mark Ward, Sr.

Through this book, 70 personal stories of faith and victory were shared by Native Americans who faced 10 problem areas common to Native Americans. There is no way to know how many lives have been touched, encouraged and changed through the testimony and faithfulness of Joe and Gerri – to God be the Glory.

September 2, 1985 was one of our memorable days at the Mission when KNMI began broadcasting 24 hours per day! That was quite a commitment considering the fact that in those days you had to have a person in the studio monitoring the equipment and spinning the vinyl records. Today, many of our broadcast hours are produced through "voice-tracking," where our D.J.s come into the studio and record their comments that will be played between songs later in the day or evening. This is a tremendous savings considering the fact that a five-hour shift can be "voice-tracked" in about an hour.

With the expanded hours of the station, more D.J.s were needed. Johnny Johnson, a former gang member from Santa Fe, led a violent life on the streets prior to his salvation. He could write his own book of his adventures that led him to alcoholism and attempted suicide. As a new believer, Johnny was a regular visitor to our Christian Bookstore.

It was there that Mark asked him about hosting our Morning Show. He readily accepted the challenge and quickly garnered a host of listeners. Johnny, although built like a tank, had a heart of compassion to anyone who was in need. And, our listeners soon found out that he was a prayer warrior. Day after day the phone would ring with people wanting prayer. On many occasions he would be invited to their homes or place of work to minister God's hope and deliverance.

Then there was another John. John Alafonso turned the darkness into light for listeners who tuned in from midnight to 6 a.m. He realized that he was God's representative on the air waves to those who had to work at night or, for some reason, couldn't sleep. His show "Nite-Glow" connected many to Jesus. He said, "The very first night a guy called in who was very angry. I shared some scripture with him and we decided to meet for breakfast in the morning. Afterwards he accepted the Lord right there in the pickup truck!" These kinds of stories were shared by John on a regular basis during his years with us. Truly, God was using this new ministry, KNMI radio, to reach those who would never set foot in a church.

January 17 and 18, 1986 was historic as the ENTIRE Bible in the Navajo language was dedicated in both Window Rock, Arizona and Farmington, New Mexico. It was 1956 when through the help of Wycliffe Bible Translators the Navajos first received the New Testament in their own language. Then it was time for the Navajo Bible Translators, an independent group in Farmington, headed by our friend and eventually mission board member, David Tutt, to work on the translation of the entire Bible.

Vice Chairman of the Navajo Nation, Edward T. Begay, challenged the crowd gathered for the dedication at the Navajo Nation headquarters in Window Rock, "Regardless of our background, John 3:16 is for us. God loved the world." It was our privilege to distribute thousands of these Bibles to Navajo believers across the Navajo Nation. Even those who could not read their own language treasured their very own copy of *Diyin God Bizaad* (God's Word). We also printed Navajo song books and "Learn to Read Navajo" booklets.

Christmas outreach to needy families was a special time for us. The first couple of years we loaded up the pickup truck and van with blankets, Navajo Bibles, fruit, canned goods and coats and accompanied Jack as we visited a home church several miles from Farmington in the Navajo Nation. Sometimes we would also go to a mission church in Bisti about 30 miles from town and do the same. I kept wondering if there was a better way of reaching the neediest Navajo families in more remote areas with tangible gifts.

So, I initiated something we called Christmas Care-A-Vans. Each of the four homes for children, along with their houseparents, would pack up the kids and a second vehicle filled with food, blankets, Bibles, toys, etc. We would go various directions on the two Saturdays before Christmas. A Navajo pastor or Social Worker would join us, showing where the greatest needs were. This provided experiences for our kids as they learned to give to others while also spending some time on the reservation lands where running water and electricity was not common. Many times singing carols and praying for those in need was an emotional, and sometimes tearful, experience.

We would always encourage our children to pack up a box of toys, stuffed animals or games from their personal belongings they no longer played with, in order to share some of their things with the children we would visit. The year before Lisa got married, she decided to go along with us and give away some of the things she had accumulated over her childhood.

Although they were now adults, Lisa, David and Geri accompanied us on that cold, wintery day. We visited several homes before we pulled up in front of a small cinder block, two-room home. A little girl's face was pressed against the window and we could hear her saying, "Christmas is coming, Christmas is coming." We entered the humble home and were greeted by the little girl and her young mother. Handing her blankets, food and coats, Lisa left the house to get some things from our van for the little girl.

As our group huddled in a corner to sing some carols, the door opened and Lisa re-entered the home. And then it happened–right there in the middle of "Oh, Little Town of Bethlehem," tears began running down my face. Lisa handed the little girl a doll wrapped in a blanket. Without knowing it, Lisa was giving the little girl her first doll, one we had given her on her first Christmas in 1971, in Willow Street, Pennsylvania. My mind flashed back to that first Christmas and the joy we felt being parents to this precious baby girl. In my heart, I marveled at how God could orchestrate what was happening before my eyes. My heart was so overwhelmed by the awesome plans of God and how he had used our family to touch the lives of others.

As we left the home, Lisa asked why I was crying. I told her about the doll and the first Christmas we gave it to her. Then tears began streaming down her face, too, as we all got back into our vans. At each stop, we would briefly discuss what had taken place. Lisa expressed her regret over not knowing the significance of the doll in her own life, saying she wouldn't have given it away, if she had known it was her first doll.

As was our practice, we finally pulled our vehicles into a clearing along the road and got out our picnic lunch to share together. Having had enough of tears and conversation about the doll, Dave decided to lighten the moment with his words of wisdom. Looking at his sister, he said, "Don't worry about it. She's probably already dropped it outside and the dogs are chewing on it." We didn't know if we wanted to laugh or cry, but suddenly Jim brought our hearts and minds together as he said, "I think if God could give His only Son, flesh and blood, Jesus, to us, and the world, on the first Christmas day, we can give up a doll of plastic and cloth to bring joy to a little girl." Our focus was changed instantly and this memory of Christmas Care-A-Vans has remained my favorite Christmas experience of all times.

For a few years, the subject would come up at Christmas time with our houseparents. "We should present a 'Live Nativity' by the children living at the Children's Home." And, just about as quickly we would agree that it would be too much work during a very busy time of the year. But, as 1985 came to a close we pushed through the "what ifs" and decided to make it happen.

For two nights on December 22nd and 23rd from 6-8 p.m., our children dressed in traditional Navajo outfits, took their places behind our headquarters building at the front of the property. A brush arbor was erected. Bales of straw formed a comfortable surrounding for Mary, Joseph and the real baby wrapped in a colorful blanket tucked in a cradle board. The little shepherds and wise men were surrounded by live animals from our small ranch program. Hundreds of carloads of people greeted by our little "angels" drove through the grounds on those two nights. The local NBC affiliate TV station covered the event and reported it state-wide that night.

One year we decided to add a new dimension. We had one of our housedads dress up as Santa Claus and had him kneeling in front of the manger for the two hours. We included a hand-out to each vehicle, "What is Santa doing at the Nativity?" In the flyer, we emphasized the fact that, "at the name of Jesus, every knee should bow, in heaven and on earth and under the earth, and every tongue confess that Jesus Christ is Lord, to the glory of God the Father." (Philippians 2: 10,11) While the message was great, the toll it took on our housedad was substantial as he tried to get up and walk following the two hours of kneeling in sub-freezing temperatures. So, we decided to forego Santa in future Nativities.

Thirty years later the Live Nativity continues to be a "night to remember" for both our children and the many visitors who drive through the grounds on December 23rd. Our "living Christmas card" now includes a route that takes people by the homes for children on the lower level of our campus. It circles the gazebo where Navajo choirs sing carols in the Navajo language. Every year we see many of our former kids show up on Nativity night with their children. They enjoy telling their children of the parts they use to play on cold, and sometimes snowy, evenings. This event has remained a Farmington tradition for many families over the past three decades.

The spring of 1986 was a special one for our family and the Mission. This was the first time we had six students graduate from high school. Our two Navajo girls, Valerie and Geri, who had lived with us since they were 6 and 7 years old, were two of them. Graduating with them were Jack and Betty Drake's two daughters, Dee Dee and Kathy and Bob and Leslie Fitz's son, Richard, and one of their foster boys, Donavin. It was quite a celebration for all of us and we were so proud of these young people who were now ready to enter college and the work-force. Valerie went on to Cosmetology School, Geri went to the Art Institute of Houston, to become a Graphic Designer. Richard went into the military. Shortly after graduation,

Dee Dee went to Papua New Guinea to do missions work, Donavin moved to Iowa and Kathy remained in Farmington, working at the Mission.

On Mother's Day in 1987, I tried to come up with ways to show Kay my appreciation to her for all the challenges she faced day after day with a large family of children. And, of course, I wanted to wish my own mother a happy day, too. I tried to call her a couple of times that Sunday afternoon, but that was back when the phone lines would fill up and the "try again" message would be repeated. The day got busy and till I thought of calling mom again, it was too late with the two-hour time difference. So, I decided to call her on Monday.

It was just after 6 a.m. on Monday morning when our phone rang. It was my brother Gene telling me that dad had a severe heart attack and was on the way to the hospital. Less than an hour later he called back with the news that dad had died. He would have been 80 years old in a few months. He had lived a happy, energetic life and taught us all how to work hard and serve God joyfully. I certainly felt remorse at not calling mom on Mother's Day. Had I done so I would have also gotten to talk to dad one last time. I grieved losing not only my dad but also my great "prayer warrior." We were so thankful to friends who provided funds for all four of us to get to Pennsylvania for the funeral. This would be the first of our four parents who would go on to be with Jesus during our years in Farmington.

Another couple to hear the call to serve as houseparents was Randy and Debbie Joslin. The Joslins had come to Navajo Missions for two consecutive summers, each time bringing a group of teens to teach Vacation Bible School on the reservation. Although serving as Youth

Pastors in Carlsbad, New Mexico, they were beginning to sense God was calling them to Farmington. When the door of opportunity opened for a position of houseparents, Randy and Debbie responded.

Within one month of their arrival, the Joslins added seven Navajo children to their two children, Tiffany and Eric. They had hearts of compassion for children and were committed to sharing God's love with those brought to their home. Debbie was spontaneous and fun-loving, making her home a great environment for their children. With the gift of hospitality, she made the natural parents of her foster children feel welcomed whenever they came to visit. Her home also served as a hub for other housemoms to gather and visit.

Randy had a heart to serve and was very sensitive to people's feelings. He had a reserved strength that offered security to the children and friendship to the staff. Being a pastor at heart, Randy found ministry to be second nature. Besides serving as housedad, Randy also served as Operations Manager for KNMI. This was his second time to work at KNMI. Three years earlier, the Joslins were serving as associate pastors in Farmington. Randy had hosted an evening program geared to youth called, "Nite-Light" that featured Contemporary Christian music that was becoming quite popular with our younger listeners. It was a perfect fit to have Randy back at KNMI.

Debbie also had a heart of empathy, which allowed her to minister to the broken. I will never forget the day she stopped by for a visit. We had just returned from Pennsylvania after the death of Jim's father. My heart was broken, and grief seemed to consume me. Debbie stopped by to talk about our trip and offer her support. Together we sat on the couch and Debbie quietly prayed and cried with me. No words were spoken that I remember, but her kindness and compassion reached deep into my soul and brought strength and healing to me.

Now, 30 years later, Randy and Debbie remain two of our closest friends. Randy has been senior pastor of Trinity Assembly of God, now known as The Oasis Ministries, for over 25 years. Debbie is still passionate about children, the unborn, serving as Executive Director of Grace Place Pregnancy Center.

Later on that summer we needed a new couple to replace Bob and Leslie Fitz. During their five years as houseparents, their adopted son, Chris, had been diagnosed with Muscular Dystrophy. Chris was becoming more immobile and Bob and Leslie were realizing he would soon be wheelchair bound, requiring more time and care than they could provide if they continued as houseparents. Although they left their positions as houseparents, Bob continued on staff as our Director of Administration. Leslie would spend several years as our Director of Development before accepting the position of Manager at our local hospital's Hospitality House.

Rick and Paula Terpsma contacted us indicating their interest in fulfilling the position for houseparents. There was only one problem. They were working at a mission in distant Alaska! While we required potential couples to come for personal interviews, the distance and cost of Rick and Paula getting here were prohibitive. After contacting their references, which included some from a nearby mission school in New Mexico, we stepped out in faith and offered them the position.

This dedicated couple proved to be everything their references said they would be. Quiet, reserved and full of mercy and grace, Rick and Paula fit right into a home filled with children. Their servant hearts were expressed through their willingness to do anything that was asked of them. Their easy-going personalities made them immediate friends and we found it a great joy to serve with them as houseparents. They provided dozens of children with a warm, happy home, building friendships that would last into adulthood. Now, nearly 28 years later, Rick and Paula still offer a hug and prayer to grown children who return for a visit. Their home is always open and we are privileged to call them our friends.

Tragically, it was around this time that Betty Drake began showing early signs of dementia. Before long she was diagnosed with Alzheimer's disease. This was a difficult time for Kay and me as we watched Betty's ability to care for herself decline on a daily basis. As Jack became more involved in Betty's care, his available time in the office decreased, too. After much prayer, Jack decided to retire as President in 1987. It became necessary for me to become more involved in the operation of the Mission, which required me to do more of the representation and fund-raising for the organization. New responsibilities also included occasional out-of-town trips, which meant Kay needed to stay behind and care for a houseful of children by herself.

I vividly remember one of those nights when she called me to report one of our children had run away. Fortunately, he returned home the next morning, but the conflict of leading this growing Mission and still caring for a unique family of 10 children was becoming a challenge. I was feeling overwhelmed and knew I could not continue to do both jobs for long.

The 1980s proved to be a time of tremendous growth and development at the Mission. We were blessed beyond words that God would allow us to see His hand of blessings up close and personal. While it appeared that our days of houseparenting were coming to a close, we believed that God still had other ways for us to be of service to Navajo families through Navajo Missions.

Chapter Fifteen

PEOPLE, PLACES AND SHOO-FLY PIE

A s we turned the corner into the final decade of the 20th century, little did we know of the many transitions that would take place with both staff members and the ministry over the next 10 years. Change is difficult at times, but a necessary occurrence that take place when a ministry is developing and growing. I remember when we finally finished our new Communication Center and moved the radio studios out of the garage, the central office out of the old print shop and bookstore building and the accounting department out of a small house.

For some of us, the comfortable surroundings of the past conflicted with the new efficient Center that we had prayed for and dedicated to God's glory. It just seemed like we were uprooting the heritage of the previous 30 years. In reality, we were just transplanting a ministry that had become "root bound." The new buildings allowed for new growth to shoot forth as we headed toward a new millennium.

Some had similar feelings when we paved the driveway and parking areas around the horseshoe shaped area that surrounded the Center. While we don't get much rain in our area, there are times when the "monsoon" rains come heavily in the late summer. It was after one of those gully washers that we noticed one of the vans was tilting and sunken about eight inches into the mud. It was time to move out of the "horse and wagon days."

KNMI radio was becoming a "teenager" itself after 15 years of ministry. As this broadcast ministry grew, more staff members were added. Pat and Robin Wells joined us. Pat began as Music Director and later would replace Mark Frederick as Station Manager. His wife, Robin worked in the office, but like many of our staff couples, they too became houseparents for a season. Matt and Joanna Sheek moved here from the Midwest. While serving as houseparents, Matt also hosted a daily show on KNMI called "Back on Track." He was our first D.J. who was a trained broadcaster with a "golden-tongued" radio voice.

Jeff Goss came to minister in Navajoland and joined the station as Operations Manager and evening D.J. He knew that the "joy of the Lord is our strength" and reached the youth with a message that they understood, leading some to Christ during his air shifts. Two decades later he would be part of the Dream Center at Joyce Meyer Ministries in St. Louis and bring teams to evangelize those in attendance at the annual Northern Navajo Nation Fair in Shiprock, New Mexico. It's interesting to note that one of our former girls who lived at the Mission has also been serving for many years in the Call Center at Joyce Meyer Ministries.

Some of our teenage youngsters had a desire to do some of the DJ work in the evenings. Byron, who came into our home when he was just 23 days old, was now in high school. In addition to being a member of the high school cross-country team, Byron loved music and had a desire to spin some of those Christian Rock-and-Roll albums during the evening broadcast hours.

I still remember the laugh that Kay and I had one Saturday evening as we were driving in town and were listening to Byron on the air. The fact that English wasn't one of his favorite subjects lends itself to what we heard him say. He picked up one of the Public Service Announcement sheets to share info about an art show that was taking place at our local community college. The announcement said that anyone with a prospectus should call a certain phone number to be entered in the contest. When Byron got to the word "prospectus" he hesitated and stammered,

" ... anyone with a pr ... pr ... prostitute should call ..." Needless to say we began laughing so hard that we had to pull the car off to the side of the road. Later that night when he came in the side door after his radio shift, he took one look at me and sheepishly smiled as I asked, "Did you have a little trouble tonight with one of those words?" He quickly said, "I didn't read it ahead of time and that was the only 'pro' word that came to mind." Those kinds of things can happen on live radio. I know I also had my share of them over the years.

Byron's cousin, Rolanda, also served as one of our DJ's during those days. Her arrival at Navajo Missions was quite unusual. She walked off the street one day to visit Byron and more importantly request a place to "call home." Things were not going well at her home and she said, "I want to be raised in a Christian environment."

Bill and Ann McKee were Rolanda's houseparents. They were just what she needed. They came to us from the Cajun swamps of Louisiana and the great outdoors of Wyoming. Coming from a colorful background themselves, they eventually were forced to trust the Lord for everything after losing most of their possessions during the oil crunch. They became solid houseparents to Rolanda and many others during their years with us.

They were steady and reliable and were especially good at dealing with the frustrations that teenagers can bring into the family dynamics. An example of that came early one Saturday morning when Bill called our home saying, "Jim, put on a pot of coffee. We need to talk about how we should handle a situation. One of the teen boys borrowed our truck last night and we just found out from his friend that they're headed west out of Albuquerque (nearly 200 miles from Farmington) on their way to California." I was amazed at their calm and sound mind in the midst of a serious crisis. We prayed together and were soon able to make contact with the boy alerting him to the fact that the state police were called and that it would be best if they turned north off the interstate and head home. The boys complied with the calm but stern request and made their way home.

Rolanda often spoke highly of her houseparents. "Dad Bill and Mom Ann really loved me no matter what I did. And, they showed me that Christ loves me, too." She went on to say, "At the Mission you have a place to come home to after school." Rolanda went on to graduate and leave the Mission for a few years. She returned in 1996 after giving birth to a little one. She then became one of our first moms in our new ministry called "Moms Too Program." She was mentored and provided direction for this next phase of her life, eventually leaving for school in Kansas. But, it wouldn't be the last time that we connected with Rolanda.

During our early years in Farmington we were surprised to learn that there were several families living here from our homeland in Pennsylvania. Dr. Ken Crider, originally from Lebanon County, became our family doctor. Jeff Bowman from York was the Parks and Rec Director in Farmington for many years. Larry and Linda Bomberger came from Lancaster County and Larry served as Director of our Farmington Senior Center for over 25 years. Larry would eventually become Chairman of the Board at Navajo Ministries in the early years of the next century. Several others also came to minister to the Navajos. And, I was surprised to see a number of Mennonite folks also living in our area.

Ben and Eunice Stoner arrived in Navajoland in 1970 from our part of the country in Pennsylvania. We quickly bonded our friendship with them as we shared our mutual liking of Pennsylvania Dutch cooking including chicken corn soup, Lebanon bologna, Whoopie Pies, Shoo-Fly pie, Tasty Cakes, Stehman's Chips and red beet eggs. But, more importantly we also came with a common desire to share the "Bread of Life" with our Navajo neighbors.

The Stoners came to serve with the Brethren in Christ Mission about an hour away from Farmington. Ben and Eunice, both musically-oriented, immersed themselves with the Navajo people and began to learn their difficult language. After the BIC Mission closed the Dormitory School, the bubbly Stoners began to work with us. For the next eight years they spent much of their days visiting

Navajo families on the reservation and teaching them to read and write their own language. They also began training pastors and leaders using the T.E.E. Biblical study program (Theological Education by Extension). The purpose was to train leaders to lead rather than training people to become leaders.

While the older Navajos were speaking English as a second language, many of the young people were losing their native tongue because Navajo was not being spoken regularly in their homes. There were other troubling statistics that have continued to plague the younger generation of Native Americans in our country.

- Suicide is five times the national average among the youth
- By the time Native youth reach 16 years of age, 55 percent have dropped out of school
- Alcoholism and drug activity has torn many families apart.
- Fathers are missing in action in many families, fracturing the stability of the home.
- Unemployment is nearly 50 percent within the Navajo Nation.

These were some of the reasons why single moms and grandparents were placing children in our homes. The Navajo Social Services department was also inquiring about our programs and looking for places of safety for their youngsters until situations improved in their natural families. The Moms Too Program was becoming more popular with single moms. Our beds were full most of the time. And, the abuse and neglect issues that precipitated many of the child placements were becoming more and more disturbing.

Our child sponsorship members were not able to provide the funds needed to provide for all the children. So, we developed a golf tournament in the late spring of 1994. The Piñon Hills Golf Course operated by our city was rated as one of the finest public golf courses in the nation. The teams quickly came together with 72 golfers participating in the two-day event that provided some necessary funds for the Children's Home.

Then, Bob Fitz, of our staff, came up with another idea to raise funds. Being an avid fly fisherman, he put together a tournament utilizing the Quality Waters of the San Juan River about 30 miles east of Farmington. World-class trout fishing is experienced all along the San Juan River in New Mexico, but the 4.25 miles of river just below Navajo Dam holds over 80,000 rainbow, brown and cutthroat trout. An average San Juan River trout is 17 inches long, but fish over 20 inches are abundant. Twenty anglers participated in that first catch-and-release Bi-Fly Fishing Tournament. The name was derived from the fact that each angler could only use two flies each day. In addition to business sponsors and participant fees, we asked each angler to get pledges per inch from their friends for the largest fish they caught. Twenty anglers fished in the first two-day tournament catching a total of 3,240 inches of trout and raised about $5,000!

God was again providing us with creative ways to help fund our care of His little ones. "Children are a gift from the Lord, they are a reward from Him." (Psalms 127:3 NLT) The golf tournaments continued to raise funds for several years until the proliferation of golf tournaments in the area lowered our attendance and funds raised. But the

Bi-Fly Fishing Tournament continued to grow and after two decades remains a very successful fund raiser with $60,000 being "netted" in 2014 alone.

Ann Connelly and Ann Holbrook or "our two Anns" as we lovingly called them, wandered across the nation leaving their homeland of New Hampshire in 1994. They packed up their earthly possessions in a rickety old RV and began what became a nine-month adventure to Navajoland. When they got into Amish Country in snowy Pennsylvania, the van caught fire and delayed their travels for a while, giving them opportunity to get some odd jobs while they awaited the repairs.

These two long-time friends believed God told them to go the Navajos, so they obeyed. They had our address from a pastor who told them about the Mission and that is what brought them onto our campus later that summer. It was their hope that their gifts and talents would fulfill specific areas of needs at the Mission. We had recently experienced the death of one of our staff members, Louise Hickmott, who had faithfully served in our mailroom. Ann C. became the much-needed office worker to run our mailroom. Ann H. filled the position for a needed assistant housemom in our homes. Both Anns eventually helped in our Moms Too Program that was later established. And eventually Ann C.'s daughter, Diane Rider, and son-in-law, John, and their family joined our staff as houseparents!

By the way, remember their lay-over in Pennsylvania? As they told their story of spending time in Lancaster County in February, we told them that we were also there visiting family at that time. Then, they said, "And, we got to go to an Amish farm auction that took place after a heavy snow fall." My eyes widened, as I said, "We also went to an Amish auction when we were there." With that they got out their snapshots and we showed them ours. We were at the same auction! And, had they asked us about coming to work with us at that time we would have told them that we had no openings. But God knew we would need them a few months later. God's perfect timing is always right on time!

December of 1995, it was time for Chris Fitz to go home to Jesus. Bob and Leslie, and all their family and friends, saw the steady decline in Chris' health over the previous years. However, he continued to cover mile after mile on his electric wheelchair, with his German Shepherd, Nikko, at his side. As long as his battery pack was charged, Chris was on the move. Shortly after his 18th birthday, on Christmas day, Chris bade farewell to this world and began walking with Jesus. A little girl at his funeral was heard saying, "I guess Jesus wanted Chris there for His birthday party." As we grieved deeply with Bob and Leslie, we had no way of knowing they were setting an example for us that would help our family walk victoriously through the valley of the shadow of death when the death of a child came to our family many years later.

Chapter Sixteen

RECONCILIATION

In 1974 (a year before we arrived in Farmington) racial tensions escalated with the brutal beating, torture and death of three Navajo men by three white teenage boys. The boys found the men in a drunken condition and took them to Choke Cherry Canyon, just north of Farmington. The men's partially burned bodies were discovered; the arrest of the teens followed. The major networks covered the marches in the streets of Farmington. Tensions were high as the American Indian Movement (AIM) converged in protest of these senseless deaths. Little Farmington had developed a racist reputation.

Now, we fast forward 22 years to September 5, 1996. A Navajo family friend of one of the murdered men came to one of our Pastors Prayer meetings that took place at the Mission. She requested a time of reconciliation prayer to be held in the canyon where the bodies were found. As she shared the details of these horrific murders with us our tears blended together and we began to make plans for the prayer gathering that would take place a couple of weeks later.

A double rainbow arched across the Mission as the caravan of vehicles left for the canyon that evening. It was a reminder that God's blessing was upon us as we headed for "healing in the hills." About 30 people gathered, including the widow of one of the men, grandson of another man and a good friend of the third one. We discovered that night that the deaths were actually not racially motivated but rather a satanic assignment. All three boys were part of the Church of Satan! The killing of a human would elevate their status within the church. Daylight gave way to darkness as testimonies were shared, songs sung and prayers offered. The lights of one of the vehicles were turned on casting eerie long shadows across the desert floor. But there was no fear because God was there with us. This land noted for satanic activity became a sanctuary of peace, hope and healing.

This was a season of reconciliation in the Four Corners area and I was thrilled to be right in the middle of it all. Since 1995 pastors began coming together in prayer as we looked at the possibility of bringing Franklin Graham to the area for a four day festival. Just before the event took place in November of 1996 we saw over 400 believers gather at the Four Corners National Monument (the only place in America where you can stand on four states at one time). Navajo leaders were present as we lifted up our region to God. At one point four pastors (a Navajo, Hispanic, African American and Anglo) joined hands in prayer while standing on all four states.

A few days later Franklin Graham and his team arrived for the exciting four days of outreach and evangelism to our area. I was privileged to serve as Prayer

Chairman for the Festival, which was held at the McGee Park Fairgrounds in the Rodeo Coliseum. I was blessed with a large group of volunteer prayer warriors, which I called the CIA (Coliseum Intercessors Association). Our team was spread out across the seats in the arena each evening and secretly prayed for those around them throughout the evening and walked to the stage with those making decisions for Christ. Over 2,000 folks made decisions during those impactful days!

Many more events took place in Navajoland during the next five years. There was prayer at the four Navajo sacred mountains beginning at Mt. Hesperus to the north symbolized with the color black. Then prayer took place at Blanca Peak (white) to the east near Alamosa, Colorado, followed by prayer teams that went to the south at Mt. Taylor (blue) near Gallup, New Mexico and finally to San Francisco Peaks (yellow) at Flagstaff, Arizona. Prayer warriors from other parts of the country gathered in Navajoland for prayer walks. Several years in a row there were Watchnight Prayer gatherings on the last day of the year. Navajo Christians organized a Proclamation Day of Prayer for the Navajo Nation in Window Rock, Arizona. Promise Keepers organized special rallies in various tribal nations including the Navajo.

Perhaps the most impactful of all of these events was the Return to the Promise reconciliation walk in the year 2000. To understand the significance of this walk we must take a walk back in history to 1864. The West was still wild and beautiful. Navajos lived in the gorgeous canyons, deserts and mountains of the Southwest. From generation to generation they lived peacefully, tending to the land of their forefathers. They herded sheep, wove rugs and raised crops for their families.

Then one day strangers appear on the horizon. They speak another language. They have a lighter color of skin. They wear soldier uniforms representing the United States government. Before long a powerful army of soldiers led by Kit Carson sweep into the villages and canyons with guns blazing. Bloodshed is severe. Anyone who resists is shot. Livestock is killed; crops burned. Even the fruit trees that grow near streams of water are destroyed. Survivors are rounded up like cattle and forced to march up to 13 miles per day for 350 miles to Fort Sumner, where they were held in cruel stockades in an area called Bosque Redondo or Hwéeldi by the Navajo. At least 200 died during the 18-day trek. Between 8,000 and 9,000 people were forced to settle on an area of 40 square miles.

Two years later, after many had died of disease and harsh living conditions, they were allowed to return to their land; a place "reserved" for them known for a long time as the Navajo Reservation. Today, this land known as the Navajo Nation is in parts of three states and encompasses 27,000 square miles. In 1868 a treaty was signed with the United States government. While ownership of the land remained in the hands of the government, the U. S. would provide health care, irrigated land and schools with compulsory attendance. The students could not speak their own language. If they did, a bar of soap would be used to remind them not to utter their Navajo words again. The boys' hair was cut to military style. Many of the children were placed in boarding schools resulting in limited access to their families. This discouraging past for the Navajos was repeated over and over again through the lives of many other American Indians in our country.

The painful memories have lingered from one generation to the next as the oral stories were shared. Remorse and bitterness has taken its toll on many of our native neighbors across the land. Perhaps Leonard Rascher, professor at Moody Bible Institute said it best ... "We as Anglos have a need to repent and Native Americans have a need to forgive." With this in mind, Earl and Cindy Crebo (who had joined our staff earlier) coordinated a Return to the Promise walk.

On March 31st of 2000, scores of Navajos, Anglos and Hispanic believers scattered out across the route of the original Long Walk and walked a few miles to 10 miles from Fort Sumner back to Canyon De Chelly in Chinle, Arizona. It was cold and rainy as a time of reconciliation was held in Ft. Sumner. Debbie Fowler, a Navajo and our first teacher of our On-Site School, said, "Fort Sumner was a beautiful time of worship and thanksgiving. This time as we walked we were returning to our land with dignity." I walked with some folks about 100 miles south of Farmington. As we headed west the winds whipped through the desert and the snow began to fall, at times plastered against my glasses. Many of us felt that the inclement weather was a good reminder of the pain and suffering that the Navajos experienced many years ago.

The next day, April 1st, rain and snow swept through Canyon De Chelly. It was in these canyons that many of the Navajos hid from the soldiers when the Long Walk began. Few would survive their relentless pursuit. Some were driven to their deaths over the 1,000 foot drop-off of the cliffs instead of being captured. It was here where we put up a tent to shelter over 200 hundred people who braved the elements and huddled together near the portable heaters for this sacred gathering. Navajo leaders were in attendance. Sam Winder, legal counsel for the Southern Ute Tribe, broke into tears as he asked forgiveness of Navajo Nation President, Kelsey Begaye. The Utes had served as scouts for the U. S. soldiers when they were searching for Navajos in the canyon.

Kay and I were privileged to participate in this historic gathering, demonstrating reconciliation in a tangible way. A few months prior to this event, Gary Foster, a direct descendent of Kit Carson, was part of a prayer journey to the top of one of the sacred mountains at Kennebec pass. He revealed that his family had two pieces of ancient pottery that were stolen from a Navajo grave in the 1940s. He had them sent to the Mission so that they could be given to President Begaye at the gathering. It was my honor to present those treasures to him as this precious time of reconciliation came to a close. There were some who took peach tree saplings into the wet, muddy canyon and gave them to a Navajo grandma to plant, symbolic of the new life that was to come to Navajoland through this tremendous day of reconciliation.

I couldn't help but think of the words that Billy Graham spoke 25 years earlier in March of 1975, to approximately 100 Native Christian leaders who came together in Albuquerque. He said, "The Native American is a sleeping giant. He is awakening. The original Americans could become the evangelists who will help win America for Christ!"

This was also a historic day for Kay and me as we reflected back 25 years to April 1, 1975, when we left Pennsylvania for Navajoland. We could hardly believe that God had allowed us to have a role in this memorable day spent with our Navajo neighbors. There were tears of joy as both young and old and various races joined hearts and spirits in unity on this special day of reconciliation, prayer and praise. Could it be that the sleeping giant was awakening?

Chapter Seventeen

FROM ONE CENTURY
TO THE NEXT

With the requests for childcare increasing in the 1990s, we realized that our existing facilities were not conducive to the kinds of children coming into our homes. Three of the homes were composed of two floors with bedrooms on both levels. Two of these homes were 40 years old and in need of repairs. Our ranch-style home where Kay and I were houseparents was much more efficient. As we looked at our existing 12 acres, we knew that much of the land on the back portion of the property could not be built on because of being in the flood plain. However, an area near the barn on the lower level was on higher ground, but not wide enough to construct the homes that would each care for 10 children.

So, some of us gathered for prayer on the land immediately to our west and asked God to go before us as we asked our neighbors who had a produce business by the street if they would be willing to sell us the lower five acres of their land adjacent to ours. The first meeting did not appear to be productive. They had no interest in making that land available to us. But, we continued to pray and ask God to soften their hearts and change their minds.

Meanwhile, we began searching for land in other areas of the county. We found some land in an area called Crouch Mesa, but it was several miles from our headquarters and would certainly create more expense to operate and less connection with our support staff, not to mention visitors who often stopped by to see the children's home. About six months later the owners of the neighboring produce business, Larry and Patricia Erickson, came to my office. Larry said, "If you can provide access to that lower land from your side of the property, we will be willing to donate those five acres to the mission." He went on to say, "I just decided to give it. No big reason, just to help. I guess God just softened my heart!" I couldn't believe the words he used … "God softened my heart." Those were the exact words I used in my prayer. God truly does answer specific prayers in specific ways.

Now we had a place to construct the new homes that were desperately needed. But, we needed to raise the necessary funds to construct these 4,500-square-foot homes. Since the beginning of this Mission in 1953, Jack Drake always trusted God to provide the funds for new projects on a cash basis. It was my desire to see the Mission grow with that same belief that if God guides, He will also provide. As the new century began I was devoted to raising the funds for the homes. Donations arrived from businesses, churches and friends both near and far.

We did not only need new buildings to provide homes for the youngsters. Some of the children we were receiving were coming from violent backgrounds of abuse and perversion. Abandonment issues were also causing concern for our houseparents. We really needed someone on staff who was trained in the area of counseling to work with our children and staff. God provided a double blessing through Bill and Linda Eubank, who both believed God called them from Houston, Texas to minister to families in the Four Corners area. They were both Licensed Professional Clinical Counselors. We quickly made room in our Communication Center for their offices, where they ministered to both our children and others in the community.

Alcohol and drugs continued to be the downfall of many of our Native brothers and sisters. While alcohol is prohibited in the Navajo Nation, the border towns of Farmington, Gallup, Page and Flagstaff remain open doors to those who suffer with addictions. So, when Robert and Rose Tso arrived in Shiprock to minister to those bound by alcohol and drugs, we were delighted to help them get connected in our community.

Robert, a Navajo, came from the barrios of Los Angeles, where he survived through his allegiances to a gang. He himself was an addict and was challenged to change his ways and moved to the Victory Home in San Antonio, run by evangelist Freddy Garcia. It was there that he found Christ and developed a heart of compassion for the addicted people that God brought his way. The Navajo Nation gave him an old abandoned building in Shiprock for his Victory Life Home. To this day we as a ministry continue to help support Robert and Rose as they reach addicted adults while we provide a place of safety for children.

There was another group of people that we believed God was calling us to reach – single moms and their children. While some mothers were not ready to be with their children, there were more and more who wanted to stay with them and get the help they needed to become supportive, caring moms. So, we started the Moms Too Program, making use of the first home built at the Mission. For many years this home was used for children, but it was no longer suitable for kids, but was well adapted for moms *with* their kids.

Earl and Cindy Crebo were our first houseparents for this program. Cindy, especially, had a desire to minister to women who had been hurt and wounded. Earl became more involved with our Navajo Nation Outreach during the day. They were a great team as we began this new discipleship ministry to moms and their little ones. We learned, however, over the next few years that it was exhausting and demanding for the houseparents who were working with up to three families at one time in one house.

KNMI continued to minister to the varied cultures of our region. Emmet Fowler, who had first worked with KNMI when he was a teenager, became our General Manager. Over the years we had welcomed many Christian artists to our community for concerts. There was one who showed a deep love for the Navajo people. So much so that he moved to the Window Rock area of the Navajo Nation and built an octagon-shaped log home called a hogan. His name was Rich Mullins.

If you don't know him, you know his award-winning song of praise, "Awesome God."

Little did we know when I interviewed him on June 6th of 1997, three months later he would be killed in a car wreck in Kansas. His response to my question of why he sang for Jesus was, "It was just something I did. It was never a decision. It was something I was raised with. I am a big believer that music is not something people ought to fuss over. The Bible commands us to sing. I believe in making a joyful noise!"

The year1997 also brought the death of my father, Parke E. Duing, Sr. After having several years of poor health, my family was faced with the declining health of my dad. At the end of a two-week speaking trip with Joe and Gerri Begay in California, we were scheduled for our last service on a Wednesday night at a church in Sun City West, Arizona. A phone call from family informed us Dad was in the hospital and not expected to make it through the night. We decided to leave on a red-eye flight following the service that evening. Words cannot describe the encouragement, strength and support we received from this small body of believers who gathered that night to hear about Navajo Missions. When Jim shared our situation and need to leave immediately following the service, the Body of Christ gathered us in their arms and prayed for my father and for us. An hour earlier, we were complete strangers. We had never ministered in this church before. Now we were family and brothers and sisters in Christ. Today, 17 years later, this family of believers, Trinity Bible Church of Sun City West, still support us with their love, prayers and finances. We are forever grateful to these precious friends.

In God's perfect plan, we were able to get into Lancaster and visit with my dad in the early morning. He would continue his stay in the hospital for several weeks, but the next 70 days would be difficult ones for him. I spent a month at home, while Jim returned to our Mission home, following a week in Pennsylvania. I knew when I left to return to Farmington, I would not see my dad alive on this earth again. Leaving was one of the hardest things I would ever do.

Weeks passed with lots of phone calls between us, but on July 10, 1997, Dad would pass away at home with my mother and brother by his side. Hearing the voice of my brother on the other end of the phone, I knew immediately my hero, my friend, my earthly example of a Godly Father, my dad was gone. Until this point in my life, no life had impacted me more, and no death had brought such grief, as the homegoing of my dad. I could not imagine life without him. For weeks and months, my life felt empty. I was numb with grief and sleep evaded my nights. I would find myself in a store, not remembering what I was there to purchase. I would walk to a parking lot, unable to remember the color of my car. For a long time, my dad's passing was the first thing that entered my mind each morning when I awoke.

With every loss, God brings us through to experience joy again. He did this for me as I began to focus on a very important event – the wedding of our daughter, Lisa. She had met a wonderful man who had brought much joy into her life, and Jami Chavez was to become a new part of our family as he and Lisa exchanged wedding vows on October 11, 1997.

While Jami was not a Christian when he and Lisa first met, Lisa let her "light shine," and one night, Jami came to our home alone and asked to talk with Jim and me. It was at our kitchen table, Jami asked about having a relationship with Jesus Christ. It was a very special evening when Jim was able to lead Jami in prayer, asking the Lord to come into his life and make him the man God wanted him to be. We not only gained a new brother in Christ that night, but the conversation that continued assured us we would also be gaining a son-in-law, if Jami received the right answer from Lisa. She said "yes" and the rest is history. I reflect on Lisa's wedding day as one of the happiest days of my life.

In the fall of 1997, Jack Drake turned 75 years old. His wife Betty, who had suffered a long battle with Alzheimer's disease, passed away. Jack had already moved from the Mission grounds to a nice home-like care center in Aztec, about 13 miles away. On the last day of 1998, God would call the founder of Navajo Missions to his home in heaven. He was the most humble man I ever met. He was my mentor ... My prayer partner ... My encourager. The list could go on and on. However, I'm sure the most important words he heard the day of his passing were from our Heavenly Father, "Well done, good and faithful, servant ... enter into the joy of your Master." (Matthew 25:21 ESV)

These words were received from one of our former Mission children when he heard of Jack's passing. "It was the past that I remember and appreciate in being associated with Navajo Missions. I'm very thankful for his wisdom and care he gave to the needy. I will truly miss his leadership, service and advice. I know the Mission will continue to carry on the hopes and dreams of Mr. Drake." And, with that challenge, I vowed to continue to do just that. To honor Jack's memory, we would go on to name the first new home built for children, "The House that Jack Built."

"Building Homes ... Restoring Families." That's what Navajo Missions was all about and that became our theme for the capital campaign to construct two new homes for children. We commissioned Navajo artist Mark Silversmith to create a brilliantly colorful painting that we could reproduce on canvas and prints, providing a gift to donors who gave to this project. This one-of-a-kind treasure featured a young Navajo mother holding her baby wrapped in a colorful Pendleton blanket. We called the painting, "New Hope," which is what these new homes would provide for many children in need.

That open field on the lower level of the campus had seen many uses over the years. It was a garden, filled mostly with weeds. There were some old abandoned wooden boxcars there that were donated at one time and used for storage. And, for quite a few years we raised pigs. The older children would have chores that included gathering up garbage from the homes in buckets and feeding the slop to the hogs. Our mission dogs soon *got wind* of this evening ritual and followed the kids to each home. As the child set down the bucket by the front door to get that home's donation, the dogs would gladly help themselves to the goodies in the bucket. The kids didn't seem to mind because then the bucket wouldn't get as heavy. Before long, we realized that the pigs had to go. Then it became a ball field for a while.

But now, it would become a "Field of Dreams" as we began to plan for the construction of at least two new homes for children. The total project would be well over $1 million. It was a big dream, but we knew we had a big God. Our goal was to have the project completed by 2003, the 50th anniversary of the Mission.

Local leaders joined our Capital Campaign committee, led by retiring CEO of San Juan Regional Medical Center, Don Carlson. Don said, "I view Navajo Missions as the 'polishing cloth' for the 'sterling silver' (the kids at risk)." Dr. John McCulloch, Boyd Scott, former mayor and New Mexico State Representative, and Thomas Atcitty, former Navajo Nation Vice President and President, were Honorary Chairmen. Tom shared, "These children need a safe place where they will have ample room, learning in a Christian family environment, giving them a good sense of direction." What a privilege it was to have a strong team of support from our community who wanted to help us make this dream become a reality.

The reality of our family life was also changing. Jim and I had become empty nesters following Lisa's wedding. Her husband, Jami, sold Dave his small trailer, which allowed our final child to leave the nest. Although moving only a few miles away, I cried when he left, knowing life would never be the same again for us as parents.

By 1998, our son, Dave, was working in the oil field. It was dangerous work and I often prayed for his safety during those long days of work. September 23 was our monthly "Day of Prayer" at the Mission, where staff signed up for half-hour segments of time throughout the day to pray in the prayer rooms.

I entered the prayer room at 9 a.m. ready for my time of prayer. There was a sheet of things to pray for concerning the Mission and I followed the list methodically. Suddenly, I felt a strong desire to pray for Dave and his safety. I uttered a quick prayer and then went back to my list of requests. Again, I felt a strong prompting to pray for Dave. This time I took notice of the time and prayed for Dave's safety and protection. I prayed for God to allow Dave to see His hand of protection over his life and experience His perfect love. The time was 9:15 a.m.

Completing my time of prayer, I went back to my office and began working. About 30 minutes later, Jim came into my office and said, "We need to go down to the hospital. Dave's been in an accident. He's being air-lifted in from the work site." Peace flooded my heart as I remembered my time with the Lord in the prayer room. I didn't know how badly Dave was injured, but I knew he was in God's hands and God was in control.

When we arrived at the hospital, we found the helicopter carrying Dave had just arrived. He was strapped to a back board, his neck supported in a brace. He was conscious, but in a lot of pain. We found out there had been an explosion at the well site. Four men were around the well head when they hit a dry pocket of gas. Sadly, one of the young men lost his life that day. Dave was thrown 15 feet in the air and 20 feet from the oil rig, landing in a patch of grass between two heavy pieces of machinery. His body was sandblasted from the sand that came up from the well. His helmet was later found in several pieces. The other two men walked away, one with minor injuries and one with none.

Before leaving Dave's side, I asked the attending nurse when they had received the call about the accident. She looked at her charts and said the first call came in at 9:20 a.m.! Immediately, I remembered my prayers being uttered at 9:15 that morning. It would be several days before I could fully process how gracious God was in allowing me, Dave's mother, to be a prayer warrior on his behalf, even when I wasn't aware of the specific danger Dave was facing.

Within a short time, friends began arriving to keep us company in the chapel of the hospital while Dave went through MRIs, X-rays and a full evaluation. God's peace remained with me, but I was eager to see Dave again and know his condition. Words cannot describe the relief I felt when we saw Dave again – this time sitting in a wheelchair, with a hint of a smile on his face. The various scenarios I had played out in my mind were gone. He would spend several days in the hospital for observation. But, by the grace of God, he was able to walk out of the hospital. Because of the injuries he sustained, Dave's days in the oil field were over.

As Dave recovered from the accident, he was faced with having to consider a new line of work. An ad in the newspaper for a nighttime supervisor in an adolescent facility caught his attention. He was hired for the position and a career of working with young people began.

Today, as a result of the accident, he lives in daily pain from four herniated discs. However, God used this experience to not only deepen Dave's relationship with Him, but to redirect his life into a career of working with troubled teens. Today, he serves as supervisor of Juvenile Probation and we are proud of the way God uses him to touch the lives of young people. This was not Dave's first near-death experience, nor would it be the last. God's hand of protection has followed Dave through a ruptured appendix, car accidents, seizure while driving a van load of kids, and, at this writing, esophageal cancer. Each experience has increased Dave's faith and love for the Lord. We are grateful for this son who puts his trust in God.

Just before the end of the century, God provided us with one more blessing … a satellite school of Farmington Schools right here on the campus of the Mission for our first through sixth graders. About a year earlier, we began discussions with Tom Sullivan, Superintendent of Farmington Public Schools, regarding concerns we had for our at-risk children getting lost in cracks in the traditional school classroom. Because of their disruptive and dysfunctional backgrounds, they came to us already a year or more behind in their reading and math skills. They were either being bullied by classmates or they had become the bullies themselves just to survive.

After discussions with the school board, it was approved for us to have an on-site classroom for our elementary-aged students. The Farmington Schools provided the curriculum and a portion of the teacher's salary. We also received Title 1 assistance that helped with the cost of a teacher's aide and computers. Because we were paying a portion of the teacher's salary, we were able to help select the teacher who would have faith values. Of course, most of the day included reading, writing and arithmetic, just like the rest of the classrooms in the district.

Our first teacher was Debbie Fowler, who decided to leave her teaching position in the traditional setting and come to the Mission to teach our precious little ones. Debbie's calm and quiet spirit produced a peaceful classroom where the students enjoyed learning. Delores Ledford was her assistant. As Navajos, they were able to connect the students to their history and culture, including the Navajo language, which is being lost by many of the younger generation. On the first day of school, August 17, 1999, the Superintendent gave his personal "seal of approval" when he arrived for a tour.

The classroom was in the former Christian Bookstore the Mission had operated for many years. When retail sales began to move to the east side of town, sales dipped and we decided to close the doors. But on this day, God opened the doors to our youngsters who desperately needed this one-on-one attention. Debbie said, "My heart's desire is to do God's will and at this time I feel it involves ministry to these Navajo children." The old bookstore was gone, but books were still being opened each day as our boys and girls thrived in this safe and comfortable environment.

A new century was upon us and exciting days were ahead for our staff and children. God continued to be on the move and we did our best to keep up with the growth He was bringing to Navajo Missions.

Chapter Eighteen

THE PAUSE THAT REFRESHES

Way back in 1929, Coca Cola came up with a phrase that quickly caught on with those who were looking for a break in the midst of a busy day. The "Pause that Refreshes" words planted the idea in Americans' minds that they could have a momentary break just by drinking a coke. The Mission board of directors believed that Kay and I could use a break after 25 years of service at the Mission. So, it was agreed upon that we should take a 90-day sabbatical.

This was a new concept for us. That term was usually used with college professors when they would go off for intensive study, research or possibly writing a book. To help us formulate this idea into our lives we visited with a couple who directed a Christian camp in nearby Colorado. They had just returned from a sabbatical and provided us with insight and suggestions. One factor they stressed was the importance of giving something tangible to the one who would fill your roll while you're gone. For him, it was turning over the reins from his horse to the one who would lead the camp in his absence.

The other issue we needed to decide was what we do while we were gone. Since we were living on campus, it would not be feasible to stay in our house and expect to have a "refreshing pause." Visitors would still come to see the Mission, street people would still knock on the door for a sandwich and water, and we would be unable to not get wrapped up in the daily activities of the Mission as they played out in front of us.

As the time of our departure came, we were filled with mixed emotions. We had been away from the Mission for a week or two at a time, but three months was a long time. We always knew we were not indispensable to the Mission, and there were very capable people to do what needed to be done in our absence. But still I struggled. Part of me grieved, like a parent leaving a child behind. (And, even though they were now adults, we were leaving our children behind, as well as the Mission). Then I would become filled with excitement as I anticipated three months without the responsibilities of caring for the Mission and being with Jim on an extended vacation.

The day finally arrived, and we were off to Florida. Bill and Ethel Snavely, friends from our home church in Pennsylvania, provided us the use of their condo in Ft. Pierce, Florida for most of the month of May. They even allowed us to use their car and drive it home to Lancaster for them at the end of our stay. Our time at the condo was relaxing and refreshing, as we walked the beaches, watched pelicans dive for fish, visited places of interest, read, slept and fell into a routine of not having to "do" something every minute of the day. We visited with long-time friends, Mark and Karen Frederick and Bob and Kim

Armstrong, who all lived in Florida. Our fellowship was filled with good food, laughs and memories of the past. It was truly a refreshing time that allowed us to reflect on the graciousness of God, the love of friends and the generosity of the Snavelys who provided this special refuge of rest.

We also visited some children's homes in the area. Victory Children's Home in Port St. Lucie, Real Life Children's Ranch in Okeechobee, and Bethesda Home for Boys (the oldest home for boys) provided us with insight into other group homes and how they functioned. Talking with their childcare teams gave us fresh ideas and valuable information about their successes, challenges and struggles as they worked with children of all ages.

On the drive to Pennsylvania, we spent an inspiring conference weekend at The Cove, Billy Graham's retreat center in Asheville, North Carolina. Being rested both physically and mentally, we were able to soak in the wonderful teachings given that weekend by Steve Brown. The Cove is a beautiful retreat in the mountains of North Carolina. A huge porch with rocking chairs provides an overlook of the mountains and fellowship with other weekend guests. Long paths are cut through the property to provide pleasant walks and times of solitude. With the teaching and music, provided by Marty Goetz, we found our lives being spiritually renewed, refreshed and reprioritized.

Then it was home to family and friends in Lancaster County, Pennsylvania. We had been anticipating this extended time of being with those we loved and those who loved us. With four weeks in the area, we were able to spend time with friends we often could not visit when just home for a week or two. We ate lots of Pennsylvania

Dutch cooking and even visited some places we had never seen while living in Pennsylvania. One of those places was a children's home only about 20 miles from where we grew up. Twenty-five years ago, when we were seeking God's place for us to serve, it never entered my mind, or Jim's, to visit this home and see if they needed houseparents. It was as if God had just blocked our minds from the knowledge of its existence. In His mercy, He showed us a straight path to Navajo Missions and didn't confuse us with the possibility and/or the desire to stay close to home.

Before we left for our sabbatical, I needed to come up with a tangible item to pass on to Bob Fitz, our Vice President. So, I looked at the square calendar pad on my desk and tore off the three months of dates and gave them to him; symbolic of handing over those 90 days to his care. The staff instructed me NOT to call home and they agreed to not calling us. But near the end of our time in Pennsylvania, our daughter called to let us know Bob had fallen off his roof and surgery was needed to relieve blood pooling in his brain! Between the fall and the surgery Bob had continued normal activities until he started bumping into doorways and having difficulty with driving, alerting Leslie of a problem. Each day he would write things of interest on the date pad for that day, planning to give the pages back to me when I returned. It was startling to see how his handwriting changed into scribbles until he finally had the much-needed surgery.

We didn't realize until we were gone how much we needed this pause in our 25-year hectic lifestyle of caring for our natural children, Lisa and Dave, in addition to our foster children, directing staff, fund-raising, building projects and even loss of parents. We were glad to get home, however, and with a second wind, we rolled up our sleeves for the challenges that lay ahead. Many times we would lean on Paul's words to the Galatians, "Let us not become weary in doing good, for at the proper time we will reap a harvest if we do not give up." (Galatians 6:9)

One of the things I appreciated about the founder, Jack Drake, was his focus on the importance of prayer. Each weekday as our staff began the day, we would gather in the office for a time of devotions. In addition to looking at God's Word, we used this time to pray for prayer requests sent in by ministry supporters and friends. Of course, we also lifted up the needs of our staff and children, too. These designated times of prayer were times to pause and allow God to refresh us for the work at hand. After the new Communication Center was built, we made use of the two Prayer Rooms located on the lower level. Once a month, we encouraged staff members to sign up for a 30-minute time of prayer, focusing on specific needs of the ministry.

One of the greatest challenges we faced as leaders of this multi-faceted ministry was finding qualified people to serve. It was not only necessary for people to feel called by God to come and serve, but it was vital for those in leadership to believe God was connecting them with us for His purposes. We didn't always get it right, but when we did, we saw God move us forward for His glory.

Tom and Annette Bauman were a couple who "just happened" to stop by for a visit with their family after visiting the Grand Canyon. A few weeks later, they were moving from Kentucky to Farmington to serve as house-parents. God took a former investment banker and his talented wife and transformed them into houseparents who would be used of God to not only care for children but also take on leadership roles that would help move us forward in our care for children. The growth of the childcare program would include the construction of two new homes for children. It was a blessing to see God bring many staff members like the Baumans our way over the years.

Friday the 13th of October, 2000 was a red-letter day as we welcomed dignitaries and friends to the official ground breaking ceremonies for the new homes for children on the lower level of the campus. Fund-raising continued. And, in the spring of 2001 earthmovers converged on the "Field of Dreams," scraped the land of the weeds and began to transform this area into a "Land of Promise."

Donations continued to arrive as our Capital Campaign committee continued to reach out to businesses and individuals. Friends from across the nation also provided resources for this important project. The cement slab was laid. The studded walls went up. The children and staff took markers and wrote scripture verses and messages on those wooden studs. Cassie Begay, who spent time as a child at the Mission, was graduating with honors from Farmington High School. She wrote, "I love the Mission. Thanks everyone for what you have done … Thanks for the 8 years to call this home." These were exciting days!

KNMI radio, in its second decade of ministry was now known as Vertical Radio, reminding our listeners that we would help to point them in the right direction. In addition to providing a contemporary music format to the younger generation of our region, we also began broadcasting high school sports, featuring the Game of the Week. And, we became the official station of the annual Connie Mack World Series featuring the best 16 to 18 year-old ball players in the country and Puerto Rico.

These week-long days and nights of games in August could now be heard all over the world through the internet at VerticalRadio.org. Listeners from the home cities of these baseball teams could now catch the excitement through our broadcasts. And, to top off the 2001 year, our station, under the leadership of Station Manager, Emmet Fowler, received the prestigious "STATION OF THE YEAR" award from the New Mexico Broadcasters Association! These were definitely thrilling times as our ministries began to expand from the Four Corners area of the nation to the four corners of the world.

In the summer of 2001 "The House that Jack Built" in memory of founder Jack Drake was officially dedicated. Before long the Bauman family moved in with their children, quickly filling the 10 beds. The second house was already under construction next door. As funds came in, the work continued. This house would be named "The House that Chris Built" in memory of Bob and Leslie Fitz's son, Chris. The little cul-de-sac that circled a play area was becoming filled with children as they enjoyed the outdoors, riding their bikes and using their roller-blades on fresh asphalt. With fall came the beauty of the leaves on the giant cottonwoods turning gold. We were so thankful for all the wonderful support we received from our community, businesses, and friends and donors across the nation, making this area an oasis for children in need.

We all remember where we were when the planes began crashing into buildings on September 11, 2001. I'm a morning person so that is when I like to pause and spend the first part of my day reading God's Word and praying for His direction as I start the day. Sometimes I will write impressions that I'm getting from this quiet time in a notebook. I don't remember the exact issue that day, but I know there were some troublesome staff conflicts that I was praying about. This is what I wrote in my journal book just after 6:30 that morning: "I know what's going on. The enemy is ticked and he will stop at nothing to bring us to our knees. There it is … we go to our knees when there is an attack, but not in submission to the enemy, but in submission to Christ who can bring us to our feet so we can then STAND!" It was right after I wrote those words that Kay called down the stairs, telling me to turn on the TV because a plane hit the World Trade Center. Shortly after I turned on the TV, I witnessed the second plane hit.

That attack on our nation caused us all to pause and realize that we weren't invincible. The Mission is close to the Farmington airport. Before long the planes no longer came and went. The silence was very strange. Our city Mayor called me and asked if I would contact the local churches and organize a rally by the flag pole at city hall on the upcoming Friday, designated by President Bush as "A Day of Remembrance." It was my honor to assist with that request and offer the closing prayer with the scores of people that gathered that day. It was a time to remember the words from Paul, "Finally, be strong in the Lord and in his mighty power. Put on the full armor of God so that you can take your stand against the devil's schemes." (Ephesians 6: 10, 11 NKJV) Whether it be an attack on us personally, our family, our church or ministry or even against America, we know that we are more than conquerors through Christ Jesus.

On January 10, 2002 Kay and I were totally surprised. Actually, it took some creative "fibbing" from Bob and Leslie to get us down to the Farmington Civic Center to meet briefly with friends of the Fitzs. Their friends were attending a conference and wanted to present us with a donation. So, not being one to turn down a donation, we hurriedly made arrangements to get to the Civic Center. We were put in a small meeting room, awaiting the couple's arrival. Before long the door burst open and in came the Mayor of the city, Bill Standley, members of the Chamber of Commerce and the Director of the Better Business Bureau who handed a bouquet of flowers to Kay. Our children were also there along with the local TV station reporter, with his camera rolling. We were confused to say the least.

As it turned out, the Chamber of Commerce had selected us to be recipients of the 2001 Humanitarians of the Year award. This was the first time the award was given to a couple. Normally, this award would be given as a surprise at the annual Chamber banquet held later in January. The only problem was that we had already made plans for a vacation trip to Florida on that date. Our staff and family knew that our plane tickets were bought and the trip couldn't be changed, so they went with plan B. Those in attendance were sworn to secrecy until the banquet a week later where the video would be shown announcing us as the winners of the award.

Needless to say, we were shocked and humbled to receive such an award. As we shared that day with those in the room, we realized this award really belonged to our staff at the ministry as they daily carry out the humanitarian deeds that include rescuing the homeless children and providing hope and assistance to our Navajo neighbors. A week later, on the night of the gala celebration in Farmington, Kay and I enjoyed a simple spaghetti meal in a tiny "mom and pop" restaurant in Florida. We were content knowing that God had called us to serve the least, the lost and the lonely. On that night 2,000 miles away, we were blessed in knowing that our capable staff would be ministering to those very people while we were gone.

The year 2002 would be a year of emotional highs and lows. On April 20, 2002, we were traveling through Oregon on a fund-raising trip with Joe and Gerri Begay. We were not prepared for the call we received that morning. Death had once again visited the family of dear friends – this time, Randy and Debbie Joslin. Their 11-year-old daughter, Heather, had passed away that morning. Nothing prepares you for this kind of news and our hearts immediately felt broken for our dear friends and their three other children. As we had done many times before, we joined with Joe and Gerri Begay to pray for Randy and Debbie and to plead God's comfort for them in the loss of their precious little girl. With her sweet spirit, curly hair and bubbly personality, Heather had been a part of the lives of all who attended Trinity Assembly of God, where her parents were pastors.

Again, we would watch the difficult process of parents, and dear friends, walk through the heartache of losing a child. We saw the grief, the relentless pain, the sorrow that etched their faces in the days and months that followed. But God owes us no explanations. He is the Potter, we are only the clay. He gives, He takes away. Knowing this, Randy and Debbie accepted this experience as another lesson in faith, believing God was not surprised by Heather's death and He would work this situation for their good, because of their love for Him. We saw their faith line up with all the teachings they had proclaimed from the pulpit on Sunday mornings. Praise God for His comfort and peace when we totally submit to Him. Their faith was a building block for our faith to rest on when unexpected grief found its way to our family within the next few years.

A month later, we had the joy of seeing our son, Dave, marry his best friend, Heather. Heather's parents also did foster care in their home, so Dave and Heather had similar experiences when it came to sharing their parents with other children. By now, Dave was working with Juvenile Probation, enjoying a new avenue of work with teenagers. We had watched their relationship grow over the past two years and had come to love Heather as a daughter.

While rather shy, Heather had gained her way into our family through her sweet smile and quiet presence. We soon found out she was a good match for Jim and Dave's wit and banter and she could respond in a quick and humorous way that put them in their places. Dave made Heather into an avid Philadelphia Eagles fan. We spent many Sunday afternoons watching football games together and getting to know Heather better. Our hearts were filled with joy on May 17, 2002, when Dave and Heather became husband and wife. It was an answer to the many prayers Jim and I had prayed for Dave to find a Godly wife to enrich his life and add joy to his days. We were experiencing God's faithfulness for every event under heaven – "A time to weep, and a time to laugh; A time to mourn, and a time to dance." (Ecclesiastes 3:4 NAS) In both our family and mission life, we were seeing God's new mercies, fresh every morning.

Chapter Nineteen

FIFTY YEARS AND COUNTING

As the Mission moved into the 21st Century, we celebrated the growth and development of the campus through the new homes for children. With the new homes on the lower level we transformed two of the former children's homes into our Moms Too program, which provided housing and discipleship to single moms who wanted to keep their children with them. For the next two years we saw many moms with children come through our homes.

While the concept was good, helping these moms get back on their feet, perhaps taking classes at the local community college or finding part-time work, it was a stressful outreach. This program took a toll on our two housemoms that were supervising each home. They had to be the "Super Moms" that would lovingly enforce the rules and keep the house in order. Needless to say, they were often not very popular in the eyes of three or four needy moms. The burn-out rate was high and after a few years we decided to terminate that program.

Another ministry began to take root and grow through the direction of Cindy Crebo. We called it Restored Warriors. This was a small group ministry that connected those who were abused in one way or another in our area. The weekly meetings helped bring restoration and healing to those who may have been affected by domestic violence, child abuse, sexual abuse and other hurtful pains from the past. This program began for women but after a year began to include sessions for men, too.

Many wonderful testimonies came from those in attendance. Here's an example. "A year ago, I would have never thought that the Lord could use my personal pain of past abuse to minister to the wounded. At that time I allowed Jesus to heal me over a 12-week period in a small group setting with other women, which transformed my life. I'm finally free of shame and guilt! The Lord revived my 'dead' heart and now I am experiencing 'life' once again."

The year 2003 was a special one as we celebrated the 50th Anniversary of the Mission. In the spring we hosted a "Homecoming 50th Reunion" where we saw many of the former children return now as adults with their children by their side. A large tent was erected next to the new homes for children. Tours were provided through the old and new homes. A barbecue picnic made it a day to remember.

In the fall we continued the celebration of our 50 years with a special guest at the Farmington Civic Center. The one and only Art Linkletter came to spin some of his great stories that he collected over his long career of working with children. Born on July 17, 1912, in Moosejaw, Saskatchewan, Canada, his biological parents abandoned him on the doorsteps of a local church. He was adopted

by an itinerant preacher and his wife, who eventually settled in California when Linkletter was 3 years old. Art
Linkletter went on to TV success by following a simple
formula: Put regular people, especially kids, in front of
the camera and let them be themselves. His shows and
a children's book spawned the TV show *"Kids Say the
Darndest Things!"*

At 90 years of age, he bounded up the stairs to the
stage at the Civic Center and provided the crowd with
constant laughter for an hour. He began saying, "In
this room I see people like I've seen across the country
who express their spontaneous joy in being able to help
those in need. You are involving your life with others.
Remember, 'a living is what we get, but a life is what we
give.' Your giving is making both your life and the one
you help invaluable. The children are our precious possessions. When you touch one of them, making their life
more valuable and meaningful, you are doing probably
the most important thing in your life."

Art continued, "I'm happy to be with you here tonight
... actually at my age I'm happy to be anywhere ... but,
to celebrate 50 years of ministry shows that this Mission
is not an 'in and outer.' Many charities begin and fail
quickly because of all the hard work and constant fund
raising. I congratulate this Mission and those who support
it for your fine work."

He closed his remarks with a little poem he wrote.
"I never want to be what I want to be, because there's
always something out there yet for me. I get a kick out
of living in the here and now, but I never want to feel
like I know the best way how. Because there's always
one hill higher, with a better view, something waiting to
be learned I never knew. So, till my days are over, never

fully fill my cup, let me go on growing ... growing up."
Art went on to live seven more years after his appearance
in Farmington. And, I try to take his advice today by continuing to grow up.

We saw many kids grow up that spent some time in
our home when we were houseparents. While some of
them came and went within a few months to a few years,
there were three children that came into our home our
first year, and stayed with us through high school. What a
privilege to see these young children grow up and mature
into young adults, just as Lisa and David had done. They
left home, chose careers, built relationships and eventually gave us the experience of being foster grandparents
to four beautiful children: Vinny, Isaiah, Byron Jr, and
Awnikah. Each one continues to hold a special place in
our hearts as they join our family gatherings and visit on
other occasions.

While it's always exciting to see things grow and
expand and flourish, there are times when we must just
persevere and remain steadfast in the work that God has
called us to do. We were now excitedly anticipating the
arrival of our first granddaughter. There were months of
uncontained joy following the announcement that Lisa
and Jami were having a baby. However, our joy would
be interrupted by the predictions of doctors that said this
little one was not well.

*Lisa and Jami were thrilled about the prospect of
becoming parents. Lisa glowed as the months went by.
Although there was no plan to have an ultrasound, Lisa
was approached by a friend who worked for another*

doctor who had just purchased a 3-D ultrasound machine. Needing a certain amount of training hours, Lisa's friend asked if she wanted to have an ultrasound and find out whether she was having a boy or a girl.

Lisa had the ultrasound and found out she was having a little girl. As soon as she left the office, her friend contacted Lisa's doctor and said, "I think Lisa Chavez is having a very sick baby." Within a couple of days, we were accompanying Lisa and Jami to Albuquerque, 180 miles away, to see a specialist. The news was devastating. We were told the baby did have problems, but the doctor wasn't ready to make a definite prediction. He threw out medical phrases, the possibility of Down Syndrome, as well as other possible problems. It was with very heavy hearts we drove the long miles back to Farmington, each of us lost in our own thoughts.

Appointments followed for Lisa and doctors decided she would need to deliver her baby at Presbyterian Hospital in Albuquerque, where the best care could be provided for Lisa and the baby. Six weeks before the baby was to be born, Lisa moved into the hospital in Albuquerque to take up residency until the baby came. Being on complete bed rest, Jami spent as much time as possible with her, often working during the week and spending the weekends in the hospital.

Jim and I spent most of our weekends with them, and I sometimes went down during the week to spend a night or two with Lisa. Friends would drop by for visits and Lisa's cheerful and positive attitude made the six weeks pass with an almost party-like atmosphere. We all tried to enjoy this time together and forget the concerns of what was ahead.

Just returning on a late Sunday evening, February 9th, from visiting with Lisa, the phone rang. It was Jami. He, too, had just gotten home from the 180-mile drive, only to get a call from Lisa to say the baby was on her way. We got out of bed, dressed quickly, and grabbed our still packed suitcases from the weekend. As we headed back to Albuquerque, we talked with Jami by phone and realized he was about 30 minutes ahead of us. On our way, I called our friend Diane Ritter, who was a nurse and lived with her husband, John, in Albuquerque. She assured me she would get to the hospital and be with Lisa until we were all able to get there.

Thankfully, there was little traffic on the road that time of night. We met up with Jami about two hours into the trip and followed him the rest of the way to the hospital, pulling into the parking garage in record time. Lisa, and newly-born Breann Nicole, were waiting for us.

The C-section delivery had gone well, Lisa was doing great, and Breann looked the picture of health to us. The doctor told us Breann's spleen and liver were enlarged and they were keeping her for a few days for observation. But by the end of the week, Jami was able to take his little family from the hospital. Because of the long drive, it was decided we would all stay in a motel for the weekend, just in case there was a need to return Breann to the hospital. Dave and Heather joined us for the weekend and we all took turns loving on our newest family member.

For months, we watched Breann grow, still observing her enlarged belly. There was some talk from doctors that she would grow into the size of her belly, but there was also concern there could be a serious problem. Jami and Lisa were referred to a liver specialist who examined Breann several times throughout the first year of her life. Without a clear diagnosis it was easy to convince ourselves she was healthy and would continue to grow, reaching all her baby milestones.

There was a bright spot during this time when we found out Dave and Heather were going to have a baby. Christmas, 2003, they announced it would be a little girl, and I began looking forward to seeing these two little girls grow up together. We anticipated the baby's arrival and on April 28, 2004, Seattle Renee came into our family. Dave and Heather became great parents and we enjoyed being grandparents to this feisty little redhead. As Seattle grew, our little Breann declined. In the next 18 months, Seattle would become a little helper to Breann, offering her a drink, sharing a toy, or just laying with her on the floor. Their friendship was tender, but heartbreaking, to watch.

Niemann Pick is a storage disease causing fat to be stored in the liver, spleen, and eventually other vital organs. This explained Breann's extended belly. It also explained why she was still not walking and talking. The diagnosis at 14 months was crushing to all of us. We were told there was no cure for Niemann Pick and Breann's life span was uncertain. Being a very rare disease, the doctor did not have a lot of experience with Niemann Pick patients. Lisa and Jami would begin getting as much information and education on the disease as possible, helping them to know what the future would hold and how to best care for Breann.

Following her diagnosis, Breann began receiving therapy and stole the hearts of all those who worked with her. She was blessed with gracious, loving therapists who were also a great support to Lisa and Jami. Being from a small community, Jami and Lisa also had encouraging support from the wonderful people who lived in Turley, New Mexico, 30 minutes east of Farmington. People were drawn to Breann by her sweet smile and the quiet way she watched what was going on around her.

Wanting to stay at home with Breann as much as possible, Lisa gave up her job of cleaning office buildings during early morning hours while Jami was home to care for Breann. Lisa began making candles as a way of making some income for the family, while caring for Breann. Eventually, Willow Wicks was born. Breann would enjoy watching her mommy work on candles and spa products as she played on the floor or sat in her wheelchair. I know the care Breann received from Lisa and Jami during her short life enabled her to enjoy life by receiving more nurturing love, joy and fun experiences than many children experience their entire childhood.

Make-A-Wish Foundation provided Breann with a hot tub, since water therapy was a way for Breann to relax her body. She loved floating in the warm water and found relief from pain during days when her body was hurting. Bob Fitz gathered a small crew together and attached a room to the garage, surrounding the hot tub with large windows and wood-paneled walls. This became a favorite spot for Breann on a regular basis. Whenever she was carried into the room, and she heard the hot tub being turned on, a smile would cross her face. Her smile was truly worth a thousand words.

We were able to celebrate three birthdays with Breann, before Niemann Pick Disease took her life on June 8, 2006. Ironically, this was the birthday of Diane Ritter, our friend and nurse who was with Lisa when Breann was born. Both Jami's family and our family spent much of the last two weeks of Breann's life at Lisa and Jami's *home. Knowing the time was near for Breann to leave us, Lisa and Jami made sure we all had time to give our final goodbyes to Breann. Their desire was to remain at home alone with Breann, during her final hours.*

Breann's viewing was attended by so many friends and family. Breann looked like a little princess with her hair in beautiful ringlets that circled her face and fell over her shoulders. A few small white flowers lay in the curls. This special touch, provided by Lisa's loving friend and beautician, was just one of so many thoughtful acts of kindness that blessed our family in those days. Breann also wore a pair of white Nike sneakers, a gift from her Uncle Dave, which she never got to walk or run in. But we took comfort in knowing she was now walking with Jesus and running through the streets of Heaven – completely whole.

Breann was buried at a small cemetery in Turley, just a walking distance from Lisa and Jami's home. Family and friends surrounded our family as we grieved the loss of Breann. My sister and mother were able to be with us during this time, returning to Pennsylvania the day after Breann's funeral.

Persevere is the key word for the National Niemann Pick Foundation. It is the best word to describe what parents of special-needs children have to do, one day at a time. It is what describes the lives of children who are affected by this debilitating disease, and their healthy siblings who struggle with the guilt of not having the disease. Because of their love for these children and their families, along with a desire to keep Breann's memory alive, Jami and Lisa began Ducks for Bucks in 2007. This yearly fundraiser hosted a day of family fun, including games, face painting, a bouncy house, live music and a rubber *duck race, with over 800 shiny, yellow ducks racing down a canal each year. Raising well over $100,000 in seven years, Ducks for Bucks has helped families through the financial and emotional struggles they experience while battling Niemann Pick Disease. Lisa also serves on the board of the National Niemann Pick Foundation.*

We would find it took great perseverance to face each day after Breann's homegoing. In the weeks, months and even years that followed, we would watch Lisa and Jami persevere through the pains of Mother's days, Father's days, birthdays and every day without their precious daughter. We drew strength from one another and trusted God's infinite mercy and grace to carry us through. In His faithfulness, He continues to do so.

Emmet Fowler, who had served as General Manager of the radio station for several years, had taken on the role of Worship pastor at The Oasis church in town. As the station celebrated 25 years of ministry, Johnny Curry took over the leadership position at the station. For the next few years he continued to provide programming that reached the young families in our region.

While KNMI was the first Christian station in the Four Corners area, there were other Christian stations that began broadcasting, too. Since they were offering Bible teaching programs and inspirational-style Christian music, we believed that God was directing us to become a Contemporary Christian music station. It was during that time that we branded the station as Vertical Radio, "pointing listeners in the right direction." Before long we got the word that our station was ranked number 2 in the region out of 17 other stations! God was truly blessing this little listener-supported station and we were delighted to have capable leadership during these years of growth.

We were also blessed with many friends over the years who served on our Board of Directors, Advisory Councils and other committees. One of those community friends was Larry Bomberger, who joined our Board in 2005. He was one of those Lancaster County folks who made their way to the Farmington area, serving for a few years at the Navajo Brethren in Christ Mission. Then he joined the staff at the Farmington Senior Center. Before long he was promoted to Director of the Senior Center. He always said, "I have never, ever told anyone that I work with 'old' people. I work with people who have been younger longer than I have been." Larry has served as Chairman of the Board since 2009 and is just one of the many examples of professional men and women who have served in these ways. And, Larry and I have enjoyed talking about some of our favorite foods from back home, like shoo-fly pie, ham loaf and chicken corn soup.

Chapter Twenty

VISITORS PROVIDE VISION

O ver the years it has been my privilege to meet lots of interesting people who came and went through our Mission campus. Of course many of the musicians who came to perform in concerts would often come by for a visit with the children. Some would have time to be on my radio show, Four Corners Spotlight. Some of these included Dino, the pianist, Petra, White Heart, The Rambos, Grady Nutt (Hee Haw show), Doug Oldham, Jacki Velasquez, Rich Mullens, Don Francisco, and on and on.

Then, for several years the Mission became the official sponsor of the annual Baccalaureate program for the Farmington High School seniors. Since the event was not sponsored by the school, we, along with the help of area youth pastors, were able to bring in some exciting Christian speakers to speak in the school gymnasium. Karl Mecklenburg of the Denver Broncos, professional wrestler Ted DiBiase, "The Million-Dollar Man," the World's Strongest Man, Dennis Rogers and Darrell Scott, father to

Rachael Scott, who was killed at Columbine High School, were just some of those that we had the opportunity to meet over the years and, more importantly, see them reach thousands of people with the hope of Jesus.

In addition to meeting famous people like those mentioned, I was very honored to highlight the stories of a few of the heroic Navajo CodeTalkers either in our Navajo Neighbors magazine or on my radio show. One of those was Farmington resident, Wilfred Billey, one of the original 29 Code Talkers. These men memorized an elaborate alphabet code, which had several variations of each letter, all based upon the Navajo language. There were roughly 500 "new" words that the Navajos had to learn and adapt into their language. The code was kept a secret until former President Lyndon Johnson recognized their efforts in 1971.

Wilfred said, "Many of my fellow marines lost their lives before they had a chance to use the code. Thank God I am a survivor!" He helped to design a gold medal that President George W. Bush presented to four of the original 29 at a ceremony in Washington on July 26, 2001. His wording in Navajo said, "The Navajo language assisted the military forces to defeat the enemy." He said he went to the ceremony for two reasons: "One for historical purposes, and the other reason to see if they really engraved my words." They did. And Wilfred was pleased.

Wilfred Billey became a Christian at Navajo Methodist Mission School, where he met a young teacher named Jack Drake. Jack, of course, would go on to become founder of Navajo Missions. Wilfred actually did some interpreting for "The Big Missionary." Billey says, "Jack and I were good friends. He was a good man." In 2002 Billey carried the Olympic Torch two tenths of a mile through majestic Monument Valley as it made its way to the Winter Olympics in Salt Lake City. Just before Christmas in 2013, I attended the funeral service of this 91-year-old Navajo warrior who returned to his Creator in heaven. That's where he would hear the words we all wish to hear some day; words that will not need a special code ... "Well done, good and faithful servant!" (Matthew 25:21 ESV)

As we approached the mid-point of the 2000 decade, we realized that many people who supported us and prayed for us were surprised when they actually came for a visit and saw that we were not a little church mission down a dirt road in the middle of the desert. We were in the growing city of Farmington, with 45,000 residents, and located in San Juan County, with a population more than 125,000. A five-lane highway called West Main Street brought thousands of cars and trucks streaming by our entrance each day. We were definitely not out in the middle of nowhere; however, there were some who joke "It's not the end of the world, but you can see it from there!"

We knew that those of our supporters who came to visit us on their way to the beautiful scenery found in Monument Valley, Canyon De Chelly, Painted Desert and Grand Canyon, were quite impressed with what we were able to accomplish with limited funds. Some have suggested we "stretch a dollar like a rubber band!" Many who came for our Navajoland Tours would often tell us, "After seeing all the beautiful sites, it was our time spent with the children that was the highlight of our week."

With that in mind, we connected with a Christian marketing organization in Denver who came and spent some time with our board, staff and community leaders. It was through the results of those meetings that we decided to make some changes that would better communicate who we are and what we are doing here. If we were going to see positive growth and change, we could not go on, as Albert Einstein once said, "doing the same things over and over while expecting different outcomes. That's insanity."

One of the changes we made was subtle but significant. We decided that changing the name from Navajo Missions to Navajo Ministries, better identified ourselves to both our national supporters and here locally. This included the design of a new logo that included both cultural and spiritual features. We even commissioned a Navajo rug weaver to weave a beautiful rug of the logo. Our Mission Statement was also adjusted to: *Providing hope and restoration to families in the Four Corners region through programs that establish self-sufficiency, resilience and Christian values.*

We also began the process of creating a new Web Site that would reflect our ministries clearly and educate the visitors to our site with the beauty and culture of the Diné, the Navajo. We even provided opportunities for the Navajo language to be heard with the click of a mouse. All of our brochures became identifiable with our new logo, too. And, the most visible change was our new and improved Navajo Neighbors publication. It would no longer be a newspaper print, but now a 16-page magazine style format that would provide sharp colorful photos and copy that would clearly portray the exciting activities that occurred through this meaningful ministry.

Our consultants were impressed with the design and interior artwork of our existing headquarters building. When guests come in our front door of the Communication

Center, they are immediately surrounded by a massive mural that wraps around the lobby, sweeping up to the second floor level. Elmer Yazzie, talented Navajo artist, took part of five summers creating the amazing paintings that reflected Navajo lifestyle, our ministry and spiritual messages sublimely worked into the murals. A traditional log hogan also graced the entrance area allowing visitors to step back in time as they stepped inside this Navajo dwelling. Two small Prayer Rooms on the lower section of this five-level Center also included murals painted by one of our former children, Geri Johnson.

With this in mind, they proposed the creation of a facility to be named the Navajo Heritage Center that would draw tourists onto our campus to learn more about the Navajo and, while they were here we would hope that they would also become interested in providing support to the various ministries that they observed. This expansion would include a museum and gift shop that would display the stories of the Long Walk, the creation of the Navajo language Bible, the outstanding arts and crafts, the impact of the Code Talkers and more.

In addition, we would construct four Bed and Breakfast Hogans. These hogans are the octagon-shaped log structures that provided shelter for Navajo families. While they were quite primitive with a small barrel with smokestack serving as a stove for cooking and heat, it was the place that Navajo families would call home. Our future hogans will not have a dirt floor or an outhouse nearby. They will be a modern version with the necessary amenities.

Speaking of home, it was about this time that we decided to provide a separate name for our childcare program. It was decided Four Corners Home for Children would most clearly relate our region and care for children. Children continued to be the "heartbeat of Navajo Ministries." After the home-going of our precious granddaughter Breann, Kay and I found ourselves in a season of grief. Kay had been serving as Director of Children and Family Services for many years, but now with the loss of Breann, she needed a new direction that wouldn't be quite as demanding of her time and emotions.

It was hard to admit to myself that I was struggling with the responsibility of supervising the childcare staff, supporting the children, assisting social workers in placing new children in our homes, and keeping up with the endless paper work that comes with caring for 25 children. It was even harder to admit this to others. I loved the work and those I worked with, but I had lost my passion and felt extremely burned out. God knew my heart. I was unable to leave this position unless it could be filled by someone who had a passion for children and would work toward providing the best of care to those God brought to our homes. In His perfect timing, He brought just the right person.

Annette Bauman, former housemother, had returned to the Mission and was co-hosting the Morning Show on KNMI. She was spontaneous and witty, providing humor and fun for our morning listeners. But children were still her first love. When asked if she would consider becoming the new Director of Children's Services, it took little time for her to say "yes!" It was a perfect fit and I felt released from this position, knowing staff and children were in great hands.

Being a former housemom, Annette could relate to the houseparents as they went through challenging days. She was loved by the children and got along well with other agency workers who came to us for assistance. Her new enthusiasm for the job was refreshing to me and we enjoyed being able to work together again. Moving back onto the Mission grounds, Annette also became my neighbor, allowing some evening visits on our porch swing as we reviewed our day. I began new responsibilities as Director of Partnership Ministries. This position allowed me to work from an office in our home, connecting with friends and donors who supported Navajo Missions and the work being done. Reducing my hours of work to 30 hours a week also allowed me some needed time to rest, be in God's Word, deal with my grief and heal from the loss our family had suffered.

Our On-Site School continued to be a wonderful addition to our care of the at-risk children who lived in our Four Corners Home for Children. We began to realize that the aging building right next to the busy highway was not conducive to the ongoing educational needs of the children. The noisy trucks were distracting and when the fire engines went by, the kids lost focus for the next 10 minutes. This building had one tiny restroom, quite inadequate for a classroom of 12–15 children. This building also included our central kitchen. Ella Woodruff has served us as cook for many years, preparing the evening meal for about 50 kids and adults who lived on the campus.

As we looked to the future growth and development of our campus, a new education center was certainly number one on the list of improvements. There was room for a new facility on the lower level of the campus next to the new homes for children. This location would provide a much safer environment for the students. This 8,000-square-foot facility would also include our Central Kitchen, a cafeteria/fellowship area in addition to an indoor recreation section that would include a ping pong table, billiards and other entertainment. Plus we would have modern bathrooms for both boys and girls!

We were looking at a projected cost of about $1.6 million to build this state-of-the art structure. With Breann's passing we decided to have gifts given in her memory to be set aside for the construction of the new school building. About $40,000 came in during those months following her death. Plans were drawn up and preparations were made for this greatly needed Education and Activity Center. Again, we realized that what God would guide, He would also provide. We were blessed to have two talented Navajo ladies, Clair Kee and Amy Dickson, serve in the roles of Director of Development during these years of transition and refocusing of our image. Their insight on Navajo culture and traditions was helpful as we moved forward.

In the spring of 2008 we surprised the children with a visit from the reigning Miss Navajo Nation, Jonathea D. Tso. After appearing on my radio show we took her to our school classroom to spend some time with the children. She was all dressed up in her traditional garments, turquoise jewelry, a sash and a fantastic heavy gauge silver crown including more turquoise and coral stones. Some of the criteria for entering the competition included being 18-25 years of age, never married with no children, speaking fluent Navajo and English, knowledgeable of Navajo culture, history and tradition. During the competition she had to butcher a sheep and demonstrate how the sheep parts are used in ceremonies. When was the last time you saw that take place in a beauty pageant?

She had inspiring words to share with our students. "Keep trying, do your best. Don't ever give up! When you have good communication within your family, you're not afraid to go to school and you make good grades. Someday you will be moms and dads and I know you will want to take good care of your children and your Navajo people. Try to speak your language. Even if you say the words wrong and your elders laugh, just keep on trying. Don't let anyone stop you from learning your language." We always were looking for positive role models like Jonathea to visit with our children and challenge them to become productive citizens.

In coming years, our children would meet the popular Navajo comedy duo, James and Ernie, who put on shows in many of the tribal lands in the country. Along with their comedy, they stress the importance of not drinking and driving and refraining from using drugs. We also had Navajo Nation President Kelsey Begaye visit with the children as he toured our facilities one day. It was vital for our children who had experienced such heartache in their young lives, to see that they too, could become restored warriors who could go on and make a difference in our world. "For I know the plans I have for you," declares the Lord, "plans to prosper you and not harm you, plans to give you hope and a future." (Jeremiah 29:11)

In the fall of 2008 another visitor came into my office one morning. This man would was on a mission to become part of this Ministry. Perhaps God was up to something that would provide a hope and vision for the future of Navajo Ministries.

Chapter Twenty One

BEHIND THE SCENES

I t was just after I finished hosting my daily radio show, Four Corners Spotlight, when Eric Fisher walked into my office. I had known Eric casually for several years. His mother was an elementary teacher for many of our kids while we were houseparents. Eric, a veteran of the newspaper business, had been on my radio show in the past when he was working with San Juan Regional Medical Center. I knew him mostly for having a wonderful deep radio voice. God got him awake the night before, and well ... here is the account of what happen in Eric's own words.

"Following about 20 years working in the newspaper business in mainly editor roles, I knew God was leading me in another direction. One day in the late summer months of 2008, I noticed an ad in The Farmington Daily Times for a Director of Development at Navajo Ministries. Ironically, I was the Managing Editor of the paper at the time ... It caught my attention for a brief moment, but then I returned to the duties of the day. At about 3 a.m. that next night, God sent me a subtle message to get up and search for Navajo Ministries on the Internet. After a few minutes of reading up on this wonderful Christian organization, I soon began to imagine myself serving there. God was directing my next life steps. The next day, I came in to visit with Jim and Kelly Karlin, the Director of Administration. I dropped off my resume, filled out an application ... and several weeks later joined the Navajo Ministries team."

September 8, 2008 Eric hit the ground running. He had one week to move into his office next door to mine before he put on his "tour-guide" hat and joined Joe and Gerri Begay and Kay and me as one of the hosts for our annual Navajoland Tour. I thought the experiences of seeing all these great tourist sites within the Navajo Nation would be an asset to his position as Director of Development. Plus, he had the opportunity to meet some of our faithful donors who came to enjoy the week with us. With his journalism degree, it was natural to have him become editor for our Navajo Neighbors magazine, too.

About two weeks after the Navajoland Tour, Kay and I were packing up for another trip. This one would take us and the Begays to the East Coast and on into New England for a speaking trip to supporting churches. While these trips were exhausting, with lots of driving and presentations, we enjoyed our time with the Begays. When visiting folks in their homes we would often have prayer with them before leaving. Joe often prayed in his Navajo language for them and that was always special, often bringing tears to the eyes our loyal friends.

Our travels back east always ended up in our home land of Lancaster County, where we held two fundraising banquets every three years. This time, in addition to sharing an update on our ministry activities, we looked forward to sharing our progress with the new Education and Activity Center project. This was good news for the many friends who had sent in contributions in Breann's memory towards the school. I didn't know then, but six years later, Eric Fisher and his wife Terri would join us at our banquets in Lancaster County.

God brought Hannah Rodden, another key team member our way the beginning of 2009. With our new and improved Navajo Neighbors magazine, we needed someone who could care for our graphic design needs, which also included the coordinated appearance of all of our brochures and communication materials. God directed her to our Web site where she learned of our need for a graphic designer. She grew up in a rural farming community in central Ohio, so the move to New Mexico was quite different for her. Kay and I admired her sacrifice of leaving family, and her courage in coming as a single person. Now, she is keeping that same Web site up to date and filled with lots of information and inspiration regarding the activities at Navajo Ministries.

I have always been amazed at how God would bring just the right people our way at just the right time to join our staff. While some may have stayed for just a short time, others would provide long-term commitments to minister with us. Vickie Franklin is one of those who joined us in 1988 working in the bookstore, then moved to receptionist and for many years now has been our Receipting Specialist. Shayne Tsosie joined us in 2000 and has been our Accounts Payable Specialist. Kelly Karlin, arriving in 2002, has provided leadership in our Accounting department serving as Director of Administration. As the years go by, these ladies have provided knowlege and reliability that is needed for a well-run office. These are only a few of the amazing 30 or so staff members who are often behind the scenes caring for all the details that keep this ministry running in an efficient way.

Rarely do we have a couple return for a second tour of duty as houseparents. Marvin and Shelia Owens had come from Alabama in 2004 to serve as houseparents. Their two sons were now adults and they felt God's leading to care for Navajo children. The Owens had spent some time in Arizona and New Mexico and had spent 50 days on a mission trip to help rebuild a church. With servant hearts and loving attitudes, Marvin and Shelia spent two years as houseparents. Their home was always open and made anyone who entered feel at home. They provided great care for the children in their home and Marvin was a wonderful asset to our maintenance team. When an emergency arose in their family, it became necessary for them to return to Alabama to help their family through a difficult time.

It was with great joy we welcomed Marvin and Shelia back to Navajo Ministries in September 2008. They fit right back in with the childcare team and it was as if they had never left. We loved this couple and were saddened when health problems demanded Marvin to slow down and not continue with the stressful schedule that comes with caring for 10 children. We are so grateful for the seasons God allowed Marvin and Shelia to serve with us.

There had been lots of historic moments during the five decades since Jack Drake broke ground for the first home for children in 1953. September 10, 2009 was another one of those memorable milestones as more than 100 local leaders and friends gathered under the big cottonwood trees on the lower level of the campus. It was the Groundbreaking Ceremony for the new Education and Activity Center that we had prayed and planned for over the previous couple of years.

Our elementary-aged students came to the microphones and recited a Bible verse in Navajo. Then they sang and signed a song that has been sung by many Native American students over the years called "Go My Son." The origin goes back in time when an Indian War Chief counseled his people in the way they should walk. He wisely told them that education is the ladder to success and happiness. "Go my son, and climb that ladder ..."

Go, my son, go and climb the ladder. Go, my son, go and earn your feather.
Go, my son, make your people proud of you. Work, my son, get an education.
Work, my son, learn a good vocation and climb, my son. Go and take a lofty view.
From on the ladder of an education, you can see to help your Indian Nation,
And reach, my son, and lift your people up with you.

Members of the Chamber of Commerce were there along with School Board members and the Superintendent of Farmington Municipal Schools. The Mayor of Farmington and CEO of San Juan County also participated. Many of them assisted with the turning of dirt. We had gathered together all the shovels we could find in the shop and sprayed gold paint on the blades to dress them up for this special occasion. I didn't realize it then, but after looking at a photo later, I noticed there were 13 shovels. Hmmm ... another Bakers' Dozen!

Two of our speakers that day included Co-Chairs of the Navajo Heritage Center Committee, Joyce Donald, Director of the local Better Business Bureau and Marshall Plummer, former Vice President of the Navajo Nation. Surprisingly, within the next four years, both of these respected leaders would pass on to their eternal reward. And, just a month after our Ground Breaking, we would lose our final parent, Kay's mom, Ruth Duing.

My mother celebrated her 90th birthday in May, 2008. Our family planned to go back to Pennsylvania and celebrate this special time with her. Only a few short weeks before, Heather had given birth to another little girl, Samantha Grace, on March 7th. This delicate little blonde-haired baby stole our hearts and my mother was beyond excited to know she would meet her new little great granddaughter. Dave's family, Lisa and Jami, and Geri and Valerie all flew into Pennsylvania to be at Grandma's party. My mother was surrounded by family and friends, making her birthday party a special time for her. With all her children, grandchildren and great grandchildren with her, her day was complete.

My mother passed away at 92 years of age. She lived in a retirement village and had a beautiful apartment that overlooked the farmland of several Amish families. I was privileged to take several trips back to Pennsylvania to visit with her during her three years spent there. As her health began to decline, my visits became more frequent. Her final weeks were spent in the care facility where she had the care and support of nurses, hospice and family. This was our only parent who we would have the privilege to be with when God called her home.

Lisa had joined us for a final visit with her grandma. My sister's son, Rick, flew into Pennsylvania from Wyoming and arrived at his grandma's bedside just moments before she passed away. As my brother, sister and I stood at her bedside, we realized we were now orphans. Even as adults, we felt the loss of no longer having the love, support, guidance and prayers of our parents. We thanked God that these gifts were shared with us from the time we were born. It is one of God's richest blessings.

By the spring of 2010, construction was moving forward on the new Education and Activity Center. The dusty field of dreams was becoming a land of promise as the concrete slab was poured, the studded walls erected and the roof set in place. As with all of our recent construction projects we gave the staff, children and other friends the opportunity to write their words of encouragement or favorite scripture verses on the wooden studs before the sheet rock covered them. Some of the words written by our students included: "The Lord is my light and my salvation. Whom shall I fear?" (Psalm 27:1 NAS) "I can do everything through him who gives me strength." (Philippians 4:13) "Your word is a lamp to my feet and a light for my path." (Psalm 119:105) Then these words from an adult: "God's got a plan for you." Perhaps these words summed up the construction of this new Center ... "Jesus–Thank you!"

It was around this time that Annette Bauman moved to Florida, leaving an opening for a new Director of Children's Services. Again, the perfect replacement for this responsibility was already on our staff. Kelly Hargrove had been working as a teacher's aide in our On-Site School for two years. Her love for the Ministry children, her excellent organizational skills, and her delightful ability to work with people made her just the right person to step into this leadership position. Just as

Annette had done, Kelly now brought new insight and ideas to our childcare program, helping Navajo Ministries to provide the best possible care for children in need.

While the Bi-Fly Fishing Tournament continued to be a good fund-raiser, we realized we needed additional funds for the Four Corners Home for Children. It seemed like the time had come to find a spring fund-raiser that would be unique and also raise awareness and funds for the children's home. It was about that time that our friend Ron Price had returned from a conference where he heard about a service club that hosted an annual "Celebrity Roast," similar to the old Dean Martin Roasts that brought together peers of a celebrity to have some fun at a banquet-type setting.

After some discussion we decided to give this new idea a try in Farmington. Our first "Roastee" in 2010 was Joyce Donald, director of the local Better Business Bureau for many years. We rented out the ballroom of our Civic Center, sold table sponsorships, got donations of all kinds for raffles and silent auctions and raised over $10,000 after expenses, that would benefit the Four Corners Home for Children. In addition to the funds raised, we were able to showcase our childcare program to many of the leaders in our community.

The second year featured the long-time President of San Juan College, Dr. Jim Henderson. Then in our third year we roasted one of the leading oil and gas producers in the region, Tom Dugan. The following year the Superintendent of Farmington Schools, Janel Ryan, agreed to the playful jabs of friends and associates. And, in the fifth year we had a hilarious night with T. Gregg Merrion, a well-known oil and gas producer, who dished out the laughs to his "roasters" at the end of the evening.

After five years we had received about $90,000 (after expenses) that would benefit the care of our precious boys and girls. We agreed that we had found an innovative fund-raiser that has filled the Civic Center Ballroom with a wide variety of guests who come together to have fun and raise funds for the kids.

As the summer of 2011 arrived I was interviewing the directors of the local Sandstone Productions on my radio show. They produce quality outdoor theatre shows each summer in an amphitheater surrounded by natural sandstone outcroppings amid pinion pines and scrub oaks. About 500 people can be seated in this lovely setting overlooking the canyons and bluffs to the east of Farmington.

The show for that summer was "Joseph and the Technicolor Dreamcoat." They had a cameo performance each night by a local unprofessional actor who would portray Jacob, speaking just six lines. At least that's what I heard when I agreed to take on that role on one of the nightly performances. As the time of performance came near, they said that actually they would prefer that I *sing* my lines. I was scheduled to put on my gown and blend in with the cast early in the summer season. Just before show time, a storm swept through the area with torrential rains and lightning. The show was canceled and I breathed a sigh of relief. A few weeks later, however, the director called, asking me to participate near the end of the summer. I agreed. After all, I still had the lines memorized.

It was a beautiful night with one of the largest crowds of the summer. I sang my lines, dramatized grief and despair when told my son Joseph was killed and later rejoiced when wrapping the colorful coat around him at the end of the show. Most of my time was spent behind the scenes observing the action that took place out of the view of the audience. Costume changes, props being put in place, along with pats on the back when a scene went well, provided me with a front row seat ... behind the scenes.

I couldn't help but think of our years at Navajo Ministries. While I was forced to be up front, and on stage many times because of my position, I was also very comfortable being on the sidelines watching others do well in their particular area of expertise. As in all successful productions, (or ministries, in our case) the "show" would not go on without all those important workers, volunteers, donors and prayer warriors who participate behind the scenes. We are the body of Christ and He joined us together for a purpose. Together, the ministry goes forward and lives are changed for eternity.

Chapter Twenty Two

TO BE CONTINUED ...

As the construction work continued on the new Education and Activity Center, the studded walls with words of encouragement and verses from God's Word were finally covered with sheetrock. Utilities were installed, heating and air conditioning along with the fire suppression system was put in place. But then we ran out of funds to complete this facility that was projected to cost about $1.6 million. The roof was on. The interior work was protected from the elements. If we could move forward with construction the contractors agreed to do the work for their original bids. If we waited for the funds, the costs would go up. If we finished the building now, we could save $300,000. Lots of options. What should we do?

This was a tough decision for me and the board. Since 1953 when Jack pitched his borrowed tent on these grounds, all construction was done on a cash basis. Two and a half years had passed since we started this project. We were in the midst of a major recession in our country and yet we believed that God would make a way to get us into this new Education and Activity Center by the time that school began in the fall of 2012. We still needed $300,000 to complete the dream.

That's it ... I thought. Let's call it *Complete the Dream*. All we needed was 300 people to make a commitment to give $1,000 over the next three years. That translated into an annual gift of $334 or a monthly gift of $28 for 36 months. By late April we had received 213 of those commitments and decided to get a short-term line of credit from our bank to finish the construction. Workers converged on the skeletal interior and began to transform the cold dark rooms and hallways into classrooms, a central kitchen, cafeteria, game room and library. The dream was moving forward!

As with most construction projects, there are some delays and glitches that occur in the final stages, which was also true with our project. So, we began school in August in the old building as the final touches were made on the interior. Our son-in-law, Jami, and our daughter, Lisa, (parents of Breann) have a painting business and provided the beautiful contrasting colors throughout the facility. Howard Harvey, a talented Navajo artist, created the outstanding mural in the hallway that recognized major donors with colorful hot air balloons floating through the canyons that border the rivers flowing through our valley. In addition, our dear Breann, whom the Center was dedicated to, was depicted in a field of daisies holding onto a bunch of helium balloons that were lifting her off her feet.

Finally on October 3, 2012, about 150 community leaders and friends gathered at the new Education and Activity Center for a grand celebration. After three years, we were ready to welcome our elementary students from the 50-year-old building by the busy highway into their new school facility on the lower level of the campus next to the homes for children.

The classroom and library were dedicated to the memory of Marshall Plummer, first Vice President of the Navajo Nation from 1991-1995. His widow, Pauline shared, "Losing Marshall in 2010 was devastating. Both our birthdays are February 25th. That was the day he got sick and died one month later. I'm so glad the classroom and library are named after him. As a social worker and on behalf of Navajo children, I know how hard it is to find a good place for these children. I love you all."

John Livingston was on leave from the Marines and showed up at the event in his breathtaking blue uniform. He shyly came to the microphone and said, "I came here when I was really young and grew up here. I attended school here from first through fifth grade and I believe this place really helped me a lot. I don't think I would be where I am today if it wasn't for the Mission and all the people here. I love coming back … I still call it home."

As we closed the ceremonies, we all went out the front door and released dozens of helium balloons in Breann's memory. It was another day to remember and reflect on the fact that God did it again! He brought people and funds together for His glory. Our family beamed with excitement, realizing Breann's life would shine on through the scores of children who would sit at the desks in this school. One day, they too would go on to become productive citizens in our region and world.

Also, around this time, Randall and Rolanda Jeffrey arrived at Navajo Ministries to serve as houseparents. This was the second time a former child returned as an adult to serve as a houseparent. John Livingston's older sister, Sonya, also served as a housemother in our House of Hope. Sonya and Rolanda were able to use their experiences growing up at Navajo Ministries to relate to the needs of the children in their care. Their knowledge made them loving, caring and understanding housemoms.

Moving back to Farmington was like coming home for Rolanda and her family. They embraced their responsibilities as houseparents with enthusiasm and welcomed over 30 children into their home over the next two years. Eventually, the Jeffreys would move into the role of Campus Coordinator and Ministry cook. Leaving their houseparenting positions was difficult, but we were grateful they would be continuing to serve at Navajo Ministries.

Remembering how Jack Drake began praying for someone to come on staff who would one day be able to take over leadership roles, Kay and I also had been praying for God's direction in bringing another one to eventually replace me as the President of the Ministry. Eric had shown his abilities in raising friends and funds over his first four years with us serving as Director of Development. Our board agreed with me that the time was right to promote Eric to Vice President in July of 2012. In addition to his gracious personality, we appreciated his commitment to God and his family and the ongoing work of Navajo Ministries.

Larry Bomberger, Board Chairman, said, "We have witnessed Eric's personal development as he embraced his role and commitment to the values and principles upheld by the ministry. We all believed this promotion was timely in this next faith-step in his Christian walk."

I have found Eric to have many of the same ideals and aspirations for Navajo Ministries that I have had over the years. He has a common-sense approach to problem solving and welcomes conversation and dialog with anyone who wishes to visit with him regarding the various outreaches of this Ministry. I know I've said it often over the years, but these were exciting days as we saw the new Education and Activity Center completed and God's leading of Eric to step into this important leadership role at Navajo Ministries.

In the fall of 2013 Devin Neeley, who had served as General Manger of Vertical Radio for the past three years, decided to get back into TV journalism. This is what he did in Tucson, Arizona prior to coming back to his home town in Farmington. Devin had worked for our station part-time prior to his college days. With his departure, we had a major challenge in finding just the right person to move the station forward in this 33rd year of broadcasting.

"But then God ... " I don't know how often I have said those words over nearly four decades of service here. Emmet Fowler had been our General Manager of the station about 11 years ago. It was then God called him as Worship Arts pastor at The Oasis Church in Farmington. I had no idea God was already speaking to Emmet about coming back to the station whenever there was an opening for General Manager.

When Emmet heard Devin was leaving KNMI, he began discussions with us about returning to the station. Emmet said he always had a heart for the station and what it represents to our community – hope, encouragement and stability. He went on to say, "I am excited to return as General Manager. My goal is to continue the vision of Vertical Radio as we reach a new generation of listeners with relevant music and programming."

After more than 60 years, God continues to move in our midst. A younger generation of leaders was joining our team to help move this ministry into another decade. While we still have some "seasoned" staff members providing crucial roles and important back-up to the younger generation of our team, I am excited to see a wide array of talented folks joining this very special ministry of hope to our Navajo neighbors.

Only God knows what new and necessary outreaches will be birthed through Navajo Ministries in the years to come. As of now, we know the Navajo Heritage Center Museum is being conceived, to celebrate the history and beauty of the Diné, the Navajo. And, if we had the funds available right now, we would expand our care of children to meet the growing demands and needs. Those expansions will take place as God provides. We have found Him to always be faithful.

It has been an honor for Kay and me to serve our Lord in this place over the past four decades. We have had a front row seat watching God's miracles take place both here on West Main Street in Farmington and throughout the Navajo Nation. God has fulfilled our dream of coming and staying at Navajo Ministries for these wonderful years. While we faced severe challenges and frustrations at times, we knew that God called us to serve in this place and do our part to help make a difference in the lives of our Navajo neighbors.

As we write these final words in the last chapter of this book of stories and experiences, we know none of these adventures in Navajoland would have been possible without God's care and provision for us, one day at a time. As the spring of 2015 arrives, we realize this begins a new "fall season" for us. On May 1, 2015, I will retire as

President of Navajo Ministries. Kay and I will step aside and welcome Eric Fisher as the new President to carry on and lead this vital outreach called Navajo Ministries into the future.

It is our desire to continue serving in a half-time role as Co-Directors of the Partnership Ministry. Through this position we will continue to communicate with our donors and friends across the country, providing updates and prayer requests, along with personal visits and presentations. We also plan to be a part of our Navajoland Tours and continue to coordinate our summer VBS teams and Christmas Connections in the Navajo Nation. I still plan to continue hosting the daily Four Corners Spotlight Show on Vertical Radio. As I have often said, "Networking is better than not working!"

In 2014, after living on the Ministries campus for 39 years, Kay and I found a 1970s ranch-style house just three miles from the Ministry headquarters in the central part of Farmington. As soon as we saw it, we were reminded of many of the brick homes in Pennsylvania. It had a country look with shuttered windows, established trees and landscaping and green grass.

It seemed like God had chosen this home just for us as we looked to the time when we would step aside in our leadership roles. We laughed at God's sense of humor when we realized the home was located on a cul-de-sac off of a street named Navajo. On my birthday on March 1, as we were moving furniture into our new home, the mailman came walking up to me. "Well, Jim, looks like you're finally moving in," he said. I wondered how he knew who I was. As I got closer to him I read his name tag. The name was a familiar one. We had him and his sister in our home for three years when we were houseparents!

We felt God's continued blessing and calling on our lives as we began our days in our new surroundings.

Throughout our walk with Christ we have found Him to be faithful as He led us from the comforts of family and friends in Pennsylvania to four decades of adventures in New Mexico. Through the valleys and the mountain tops, He led us all the way. We have found these words in Proverbs to encourage us in our journey. "Trust in the Lord with all your heart and lean not on your own understanding; in all your ways acknowledge Him, and He will make your paths straight." (Proverbs 3: 5, 6)

I don't know where I heard this, but I have it written in my Bible, and reflect on it often.

God is God – Nothing less
People are people – Nothing more
Miracles are miracles – Nothing else!

We have enjoyed sharing some of the stories that God has allowed us to experience. There have been tears of sadness and joy. I'm sure you have experienced the same. While we don't know what the future holds, we do know who holds the future. That future includes Navajo Ministries in Farmington, New Mexico. Fortunately, God's story, our story and your story does not end here. Let's just say, "TO BE CONTINUED …"

BAKERS' DOZEN OF
FAVORITE BIBLE VERSES

One thing I have asked from the Lord, this only do I seek: that I may dwell in the house of the Lord all the days of my life, to gaze on the beauty of the Lord and to seek Him in His temple. (Psalm 27:4)

Wait for the Lord; be strong and take heart and wait for the Lord. (Psalm 27: 14)

Take delight in the Lord, and He will give you the desires of your heart. (Psalm 37:4)

This is the day that the Lord has made; let us rejoice and be glad in it. (Psalm 118:24 KJV)

Children are a gift from God, they are His reward. (Psalm 127:3 NLT)

Trust in the Lord with all your heart and lean not on your own understanding; in all your ways acknowledge Him, and He will make your paths straight. (Proverbs 3:5, 6)

"For I know the plans I have for you," declares the Lord, plans to prosper you and not to harm you, plans to give you hope and a future." (Jeremiah 29:11)

Because of the Lord's great love we are not consumed, for His compassions never fail. They are new every morning; great is Your faithfulness. (Lamentations 3: 22, 23)

We are more than conquerors through Him that loved us. (Romans 8:37)

Rejoice in the Lord always. I will say it again: Rejoice! (Philippians 4:4)

I can do all things through Christ who strengthens us. (Philippians 4:13 NKJV)

If any of you lacks wisdom, he should ask God, who gives generously to all without finding fault, and it will be given to you. (James 1:5)

He will wipe every tear from their eyes. There will be no more death or mourning or crying or pain, for the old order of things has passed away. (Revelation 21:4)

CONNECTIONS

All the proceeds from the sale of this book will benefit the various outreaches of:

Navajo Ministries
2103 W. Main Street
Farmington, NM 87401

Ways that you can help:

- Provide a donation — Navajo Ministries is a 501(c)(3) Non-Profit Organization
  By Mail: Navajo Ministries, P.O. Box 1230, Farmington, NM 87499
  By Internet: Visit <u>www.NavajoMinistries.org/ giving-support/</u>
  By Phone: Toll Free – 1-888-325-0255
- Sponsor a child or family of children at the Four Corners Home for Children located at Navajo Ministries.
- Sponsor the On-Site School located on the campus of Navajo Ministries.

You can also clip Box Tops for Education and Labels for Education.

- Support the broadcast ministry of Vertical Radio located at Navajo Ministries.
- Participate in the annual Bi-Fly Fishing Tournament in the Quality Waters of the San Juan River, held each August.
- Join us for the annual Navajoland Tour. This one-week tour will include visits to Monument Valley, Four Corners Monument, Canyon De Chelly, Grand Canyon, Painted Desert, and much more, including a meal with the children.
- Sign up to receive the semi-annual Navajo Neighbors magazine.
- Sign up for the monthly Prayer Link. You will receive a list of individual prayer needs and we also encourage you to send us your requests. Our staff meets for prayer each morning.
- Find us on Facebook under Navajo Ministries or The Bakers' Dozen and Then Some.
- Remember Navajo Ministries when considering your estate planning.
- Remember a departed loved one with a gift to Navajo Ministries in their memory.

To learn more about the beginnings of Navajo
Ministries order a copy of
"THE BIG MISSIONARY"
book by founder Jack Drake.

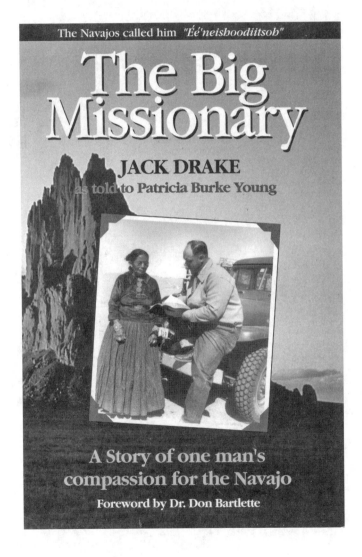